Research and Writing Guide for Political Science

Kristen P. Williams
Clark University

New York Oxford
Oxford University Press

Oxford University Press is a department of the University of Oxford. It furthers the University's objective of excellence in research, scholarship, and education by publishing worldwide.

Oxford New York
Auckland Cape Town Dar es Salaam Hong Kong Karachi
Kuala Lumpur Madrid Melbourne Mexico City Nairobi
New Delhi Shanghai Taipei Toronto

With offices in
Argentina Austria Brazil Chile Czech Republic France Greece
Guatemala Hungary Italy Japan Poland Portugal Singapore
South Korea Switzerland Thailand Turkey Ukraine Vietnam

For titles covered by Section 112 of the US Higher Education
Opportunity Act, please visit www.oup.com/us/he for the
latest information about pricing and alternate formats.

Published in the United States of America by
Oxford University Press
198 Madison Avenue, New York, NY 10016
http://www.oup.com

Oxford is a registered trade mark of Oxford University Press.

ISBN 978-0-19-989054-5

Brief Contents

Chapter 1: Introduction   1

Chapter 2: Conducting Research: Finding, Evaluating, and Using Sources   30

Chapter 3: Writing, Rewriting, Revising, and Editing   52

Chapter 4: Citations and Bibliography   70

Chapter 5: Conclusion—Further Readings   109

Bibliography   120

Contents

Chapter 1: Introduction   1

WHAT THIS BOOK DOES DO AND WHAT IT DOES NOT DO   6

WHY WRITE A RESEARCH PAPER?   8

GETTING STARTED: I HAVE TO WRITE A RESEARCH PAPER. . . .

WHAT DO I DO NEXT?   10

    Parts of a Research Paper   12

       Introduction   14

       Literature Review   17

       Research Design   23

       Evidence/Analysis: Testing Your Hypothesis   25

       Conclusion   27

       Bibliography or Works-Cited page   28

CONCLUSION   28

Chapter 2: Conducting Research: Finding, Evaluating, and Using Sources   30

SCHOLARLY SOURCES: WHAT ARE THEY?   30

    Primary and Secondary Sources   31

    Books   33

    Scholarly journals   34

    Finding Scholarly Journal Articles and Book Reviews   38

    Newspapers and magazines   41

Contents

Data and Statistical Sources   41

Internet   43

Library and the librarians   45

TAKING EFFECTIVE NOTES   46

CONCLUSION   51

Chapter 3: Writing, Rewriting, Revising, and Editing   52

WRITING: DRAFTS, DRAFTS, AND MORE DRAFTS   52

Writing the Paper   54

The Introduction   58

The Literature Review   59

REVISING   61

EDITING THE PAPER   63

THE NITTY-GRITTY: FORMATTING THE PAPER IN PREPARATION FOR

SUBMISSION   64

PROOFREADING   67

GETTING FEEDBACK FROM OTHERS   68

CONCLUSION   68

Chapter 4: Citations and Bibliography   70

CITING DIRECT QUOTES, PARAPHRASE, AND IDEAS   71

CITATION STYLES   72

APA Style and References List   73

Other things to keep in mind as you cite and write using the APA style   79

MLA Style and Works-Cited List   80

Other things to keep in mind when you cite and write using the MLA style   87

Chicago Style: Citations and Bibliography   88

Other things to keep in mind when you cite and write using the Chicago style 101

CONCLUSION   108

Chapter 5: Conclusion—Further Readings   109

Books for political science papers   110

General books on research and writing papers   115

Bibliography   120

Chapter 1

Introduction

What exactly is political science? According to the American Political Science Association, "Political science is the study of governments, public policies and political processes, systems, and political behavior. Political science subfields include political theory, political philosophy, political ideology, political economy, policy studies and analysis, comparative politics, international relations, and a host of related fields. . . . Political scientists use both humanistic and scientific perspectives and tools and a variety of methodological approaches to examine the process, systems, and political dynamics of all countries and regions of the world."[1] In essence, political scientists study a myriad of topics within countries and across countries: types of governments (democracies, authoritarian regimes), wars (how they start and how they end as well as what happens during wars), peace (negotiations, peace building, peacekeeping), economics (trade between countries; exports and imports), transitions to democracy, immigration, human rights, gender, elections, interest groups, voting behavior, public opinion, and so forth. As you can imagine, this is by no means an exhaustive list.

How do political scientists study these topics? They do so by asking research questions. Here are some examples: What role does public opinion play in American politics? How do interest groups affect foreign policy decisions? What factors led to the Russian Revolution? Why did the Soviet Union place missiles in Cuba in 1962? How can we account for the U.S. invasion of Iraq in 2003? Why did North Korea invade South Korea in June 1950? How can we explain NATO's decision to intervene in Libya in 2011? Why did the United Nations Security Council

---

[1] American Political Science Association, "What is Political Science?" accessed May 24, 2011, http://apsanet.org/content_9181.cfm?navID=727.

pass Resolution 1325, which calls for the inclusion of women in peace negotiations? These are "puzzles" that political scientists want to "solve," and they do so by conducting research to answer these questions. But political scientists do not engage in research only for themselves: they engage in research to contribute to the production of knowledge. Ask yourself: *How do we know the things that we know?* How do we know that public opinion matters in American politics? How do we know what factors mattered in the outbreak of the Russian Revolution? How do we know why Eastern European countries experienced the transition to democracy? How do we know why the Soviet Union decided to place missiles in Cuba? How do we know why North Korea invaded South Korea? How do we know why the United States decided to invade Iraq? Through conducting research scholars contribute to the production of new knowledge by asking new questions from which other scholars can learn. For other scholars to learn and contribute to yet further knowledge, they need to know what research has been done. The means by which they learn about such research consists of reading the works of other political scientists and other scholars. Thus, presenting and publishing research is part and parcel of what political scientists (as well as scholars in other disciplines, or fields of study) do. For example, in a recent issue of *International Studies Perspectives*, one of the leading academic journals in the field of international relations, the authors asked the research question: What role do international criminal tribunals and domestic human rights trials play in peace building in societies after a civil war ends? James D. Meernik, Angela Nichols, and Kimi L. King examined whether these tribunals and trials play a positive role in improving human rights and maintaining peace in such societies. They wanted to find out whether human rights actually did improve. They also wanted to find out if civil war erupted again even when international tribunals and domestic trials were present. To answer their research question, they looked at all states where a civil war ended since 1982. What they found was that although these tribunals and trials had a positive impact on the society, they did not prevent civil war from breaking out again.[2]

In another example, scholars are interested in whether weak and failing states pose a security threat to the international community. The conventional wisdom is that they do. Challenging that conventional wisdom, the author of a recent book, Stewart Patrick, analyzes several issues (such as disease, terrorism, transnational crime, and weapons of mass destruction) and finds that some transnational threats do come from weak and failing states. What he demonstrates, however, is that the citizens of those states suffer more. Thus, although there are some threats to international security, they are far outweighed by the security threats to the citizens within those states. In fact, he argues that many global threats emerge from states that are "wealthier and more stable," not the poor and weak ones.[3]

In thinking about both of these examples, the authors have asked a research question, evaluated the research done by others, proposed and tested hypotheses by using empirical evidence, and presented their own findings. From there, other scholars will do the same, building on existing knowledge to further research and knowledge. All of this is a function of the research and writing process by others. It is through the research and writing process that a community of scholars contributes to the generation of new knowledge and understanding. Thus, understanding why international wars begin comes about from studying particular wars, such as World War I or the 1973 Arab-Israeli war. Is the cause domestic politics? Is it the motivations and beliefs of particular leaders who decided to initiate war? Understanding how China may challenge U.S. dominance in the post–Cold War period comes about from studying what factors lead states to

---

[2] James D. Meernik, Angela Nichols, and Kimi L. King, "The Impact of International Tribunals and Domestic Trials on Peace and Human Rights after Civil War," *International Studies Perspectives* 11, 4 (2010): 309–34.
[3] Stewart Patrick, *Weak Links: Fragile States, Global Threats, and International Security* (New York: Oxford University Press, 2011).

rise and challenge a dominant state and what factors lead to a dominant state's decline. Perhaps a

state has experienced an increase in economic power or modernized its military. Perhaps it seeks

territory. Understanding of the way civil wars affect women comes about from studying gender

relations within a country—the socially constructed roles of men and women as members of that

society. Are women marginalized and expected to fulfill traditional roles as wives and mothers?

How are women involved in peace negotiations to end conflicts? How are women involved in

conflict as combatants?

As students in political science courses, through the professor's lectures and assigned

readings, you are exposed to the research done by others. In turn, professors want you to be part

of this community of scholars and often will assign research papers so that you can demonstrate

your knowledge and understanding of a topic. Imagine this: Your political science professor has

handed out a research paper assignment asking you to apply the major theories in international

relations (realism, liberalism, and constructivism[4]) to a topic in world politics. The assignment

requires that you evaluate the different theories and determine which one best explains that topic.

For example, you might be asked to write a paper on "Why did the IMF [International Monetary

Fund] assist South Korea during the Asian financial crisis of 1997?"[5] You would need to know

and explain what the theories are and their assumptions, as well as their limitations. You also

would need to know something about the Asian financial crisis and something about how the

---

[4] For some of the major works on realism, see John J. Mearsheimer, "The False Promise of International Institutions," *International Security* 19 (Winter 1994/1995): 5–49; Stephen M. Walt, *The Origins of Alliances* (Ithaca, NY: Cornell University Press, 1987); and Kenneth N. Waltz, *Theory of International Politics* (New York: Random House, 1979). For works on liberalism, see Michael W. Doyle, "Liberalism and World Politics," *American Political Science Review* 80 (December 1986): 1151–69; and Robert O. Keohane and Lisa L. Martin, "The Promise of Institutionalist Theory," *International Security* 20 (1995): 39–51. On constructivism, see Alexander Wendt, "Anarchy Is What States Make of It: The Social Construction of Power Politics," *International Organization* 46, 2 (Spring 1992): 391–425.
[5] Professor Nancy Lapp, research paper assignment for *International Politics* course (Government 130), California State University, Sacramento (Summer 2010).

crisis affected South Korea, and you would need to know something about the IMF's decision-making process. Given that the IMF is composed of states, what are the voting patterns?

Another assignment might involve writing a research paper that examines the origins of revolutions for which you are asked to compare and contrast the factors that explain the Russian Revolution and the French Revolution. Were the same factors present in both? You would have to know something about the historical background of these two revolutions. You would have to know something about the leaders in power at the time and those who opposed the leaders and the regimes. It might be important to examine the social and economic conditions in Russia and France at the time. What role did the nobility play? What role did the peasants play?

In yet another example, your professor has asked you to write a research paper examining the role of public opinion in American politics. In doing so, you might need to look at public opinion polls. In turn, that means discerning how polls are conducted, what pollsters actually do, in order to evaluate which are good public opinion polls and which are not. Or perhaps you are taking a course in campaign finance and are told to analyze the role of money in American elections. You would need to familiarize yourself with the various actors who matter in the American campaign finance system, such as the candidates, interest groups, individual donors, and political parties. What are their motivations for contributing money to an election? What are the motivations of the candidate who receives the financial contributions?[6]

In thinking about these examples, you might be asking yourself: What do I do first? How do I go about getting started? Where do I go to find the research? How should a paper be organized? How do I go about citing the research? What is the difference between a footnote and an endnote? What is the difference between the MLA, APA, and Chicago citation styles? What

---

[6] Course assignments on "Public Opinion and American Democracy" and "Money and Politics," for Professor Robert Boatright, Clark University.

is the difference between a bibliography, a works-cited list, and a reference list? This very short guide to writing research papers in political science is meant to answer those questions. In the chapters that follow, students will be exposed to the basic skills of research and writing a research paper.

The remainder of this chapter is divided into several sections. The next section discusses what this book does do and, equally important, what it does not do. Then the chapter asks (and answers) the question, "Why write a research paper?" Writing is a form of communication and expression of ideas and arguments. It is also a means of demonstrating critical thinking and written communication skills. The section that follows gives a detailed overview of how to get started in writing a research paper in political science, including choosing a topic and making an outline, and describes the parts of a research paper. The conclusion provides a road map for the chapters that follow.

WHAT THIS BOOK DOES DO AND WHAT IT DOES NOT DO

Many excellent books on writing research papers are available to students (undergraduate and graduate students alike). Several of these books (both for political science[7] specifically and for writing generally[8]) are listed in the concluding chapter. These books provide extensive and

---

[7] See, for example, American Political Science Association, *Style Manual for Political Science*, revised ed. (Washington, DC: American Political Science Association, 2001); Lisa A. Baglione, *Writing a Research Paper in Political Science: A Practical Guide to Inquiry, Structure, and Methods* (Belmont, CA: Thomson Wadsworth, 2007); James M. Carlson and Mark S. Hyde, *Doing Empirical Political Research* (Boston: Houghton Mifflin, 2003); Lucille Charlton and Mark Charlton, *Thomson Nelson Guide to Research and Writing in Political Science* (Toronto: Nelson, 2006); Laura Roselle and Sharon Spray, *Research and Writing in International Relations* (New York: Pearson Longman, 2008); Diane E. Schmidt, *Writing in Political Science: A Practical Guide*, 4th ed. (New York: Pearson Longman, 2010); Gregory M. Scott and Stephen M. Garrison, *The Political Science Student Writer's Manual*, 7th ed. (New York: Pearson Longman, 2012).

[8] Wayne G. Booth, Gregory G. Colomb, and Joseph M. Williams, *The Craft of Research*, 3rd ed. (Chicago: University of Chicago Press, 2008); Thomas S. Kane, *The Oxford Essential Guide to Writing* (New York: Berkley Books, 2000); Charles Lipson, *How to Write a BA Thesis: A Practical Guide from Your First Ideas to Your Finished Paper* (Chicago: University of Chicago Press, 2005); *MLA Handbook for Writers of Research Papers*, 7th ed. (New York: Modern Language Association of America, 2009); William Strunk Jr. and E. B. White, *The Elements of Style*,

comprehensive coverage of all aspects of the research and writing process and the more specific aspects of writing itself, namely, style and grammar usage (punctuation, sentence structure, etc.).

This book is also focused on the process of writing a research paper. What this book <u>does not do</u> is also important to know. It does not focus on the use of narratives, detailed descriptions of quantitative ("scientific") methods, or various types of paper assignments you might have in your political science courses apart from a research paper (honors theses, book reviews, essays, policy position papers, and so forth). The books listed in Chapter 5 are useful resources for these more detailed writing assignments.[9] This book also does not explicitly or exhaustively deal with usage of the English language, including grammar (e.g., the difference between the use of the possessive "its" and "it's," the contraction of "it is") and spelling (for example, listing frequently misused words).[10]

What this book <u>does do</u> is provide students with a <u>very basic and short</u> guide, or primer, on the nitty-gritty of how to get started writing a research paper, explain the parts of a research paper, provide suggestions for effective note taking, and present the citation formats found in academic writing. In essence, the book presents students with basic information about how to go about conducting research (finding and evaluating sources) and then writing the paper itself.

4th ed. (Needham Heights, MA: Allyn & Bacon, 2000); Kate L. Turabian, *A Manual for Writers of Research Papers, Theses, and Dissertations,* 7th ed., revised by Wayne C. Booth, Gregory G. Colomb, and Joseph M. Williams and the University of Chicago Editorial Press Staff (Chicago: University of Chicago Press, 2007); Kate L. Turabian, *Student's Guide to Writing College Papers,* 4th ed., revised by Gregory G. Colomb and Joseph M. Williams and the University of Chicago Press Editorial Staff (Chicago: University of Chicago Press, 2010).

[9] On different kinds of writing assignments in political science, see Charlton and Charlton, *Thomson Nelson Guide to Research and Writing in Political Science*; Schmidt, *Writing in Political Science*; and Scott and Garrison, *The Political Science Student Writer's Manual.*

[10] For spelling and language usage, see Joseph Gibaldi, *MLA Handbook for Writers of Research Papers,* 5th ed. (New York: Modern Language Association of America, 1999); Kane, *The Oxford Essential Guide to Writing*; Strunk and White, *The Elements of Style*; Turabian, *Student's Guide to Writing College Papers.*

WHY WRITE A RESEARCH PAPER?

Why do professors have students write research papers? What are the goals and objectives of such an endeavor? Most basically, writing research papers in political science is about asking "why" or "how" questions about various topics in the discipline. This is what political scientists do too. They write scholarly works that seek to answer important, compelling, and interesting questions about politics, broadly defined.

Writing is, in essence, a form of communication. Writers convey their ideas to others: the audience, the reader. It is because a writer is communicating ideas and knowledge to the reader that it is imperative to write clearly and effectively. You want the reader to be able to understand what you are trying to say. Unclear writing, whether for a college course, a cover letter for a job, or a report for your employer, makes it easier for the reader to dismiss what you have to say. Thus, the process of writing a research paper enables writers to demonstrate their written communication skills.

A research paper helps students develop critical thinking skills by engaging in research to answer a research question, evaluating that research in terms of developing testable hypotheses, analyzing and assessing the evidence, and formulating a conclusion that is based on the evaluation of that evidence. As Gamze Cavdar and Sue Doe assert, "Associated with higher-order thinking, critical thinking involves 'knowledge transformation' . . . rather than the kind of knowledge-telling associated with production of lists or other memorized recitals of information." Further, they argue, "Critical thinkers also demonstrate the ability to tease out the assumptions of varied approaches and then stake an informed claim or make a judgment about the approaches based on available information and a deliberate process that is both analytic and synthetic. At the same time, critical thinkers also recognize that their claims are provisional or subject to revision based on new information."[11]

Besides doing more writing, reading (and lots of it) is a wonderful way to become a better writer. Reading and seeing how authors write, how they construct sentences and their prose, is a way to learn to be a better writer, and reading others' works helps build vocabulary.

It is also important to recognize that good writing takes time—it requires one to do a lot of writing, rewriting, revising, and editing. Because good writing takes time, students need to make sure that they have good time management skills. To produce a good research paper (or other written assignments) students must be willing to devote the time and energy to the research and writing processes. Professors can tell when students have not spent sufficient time researching and writing their papers. Papers are likely to be filled with grammatical errors and typographical errors and lack organization and fluidity. To quote political scientist Stephen Van Evera, "A messy-looking paper suggests a messy mind."[12]

For all these reasons (developing critical thinking skills and written communication skills, developing good time management skills, contributing to new knowledge—all of which are important learning objectives in just about any course you take in college), writing a research paper is an important way to learn about political science. So your professor has assigned a research paper—now what?

---

[11] Gamze Cavdar and Sue Doe, "Learning Through Writing: Teaching Critical Thinking Skills in Writing Assignments," *PS: Political Science & Politics* 45, 2 (April 2012), 298–99.
[12] Stephen Van Evera, *Guide to Methods for Students of Political Science* (Ithaca, NY: Cornell University Press, 1997), 128.

GETTING STARTED: I HAVE TO WRITE A RESEARCH PAPER. . . . WHAT DO I DO NEXT?

Getting started on a research paper can be a daunting task. The thought of writing, say, a 15- to 20-page paper can leave a student feeling overwhelmed. In thinking of the research questions that political scientists might seek to answer, if you have to write a paper analyzing an international event (war, invasion, peace negotiations) using the major theories, or approaches, in international relations (realism, liberalism, and constructivism), and determining which theory best explains this event, your mind probably is already thinking: What event do I choose? How do I learn about the theories? What does it mean to apply these theories in the context of the event? How do I find evidence? What does it mean to analyze something? How will I ever write 15 pages, let alone 20 pages? The key to overcoming this feeling of being overwhelmed is to think of the paper in its constituent parts. This section is designed to do just that by discussing each part of a research paper: introduction, body, and conclusion. These parts are pretty much universal across academic disciplines, not just specific to political science. As was noted earlier, scholars ask research questions; look to the existing works on that topic; provide, analyze, and evaluate that evidence; and then formulate a conclusion, thereby contributing to further knowledge about that topic.

Some research paper assignments will be quite specific, as in the example noted above, in which a student must examine, analyze, and evaluate the main theories in international relations in terms of a particular event, such as a war or a treaty. Other research assignments might be more open-ended. For example, an assignment might ask you to write a research paper on general topics such as international military intervention in an internal (civil) war, the causes of an interstate (international) war, or the political explanations of international trade policies.[13] Or you might be asked to write a paper that answers questions such as: How does China behave as a major external actor in Africa? What is the role of terrorist groups in Africa? Why do so many Islamic revolutionary groups operate in Sudan and other African states? What are the causes of ethnic conflict in Africa?[14] In all these instances, students probably will have been assigned readings about these topics in the course. In producing a research paper that addresses these topics, students will be expected to go beyond the assigned readings to demonstrate their understanding of the course material and also be able to apply the theories they have learned. The research process is about finding scholarly sources of material that have been written on your topic and evaluating the evidence in order to answer your research question. Think of the research project as a building: the professor has provided you with the concrete foundation (the assigned readings that discuss the theories used in the course and perhaps some real-world examples), but you are required to construct the building by erecting the walls and supports, laying the floors, putting on the roof, installing the plumbing and electrical lines, installing the windows and doors, and so forth—basically completing the entire structure.

If we apply this analogy to a political science paper, consider the following example: you have been asked to choose an interstate war, determine its causes, and determine which of those causes best explain why the war started. Most likely, your professor has lectured about and assigned readings on the causes of war. Perhaps she talked about international factors (such as the balance of power), domestic factors (government type, military, foreign ministry, public

---

[13] Drawn from Professor Shale Horowitz's (University of Wisconsin, Milwaukee) syllabus for Political Science 500, *Capstone Course in Political Science* (Spring 2011), for the research paper topics that students might consider writing.
[14] These questions for assigned research papers are drawn from Professor Stephen Burgess's (Maxwell Air Force College) syllabus for his course *Regional and Cultural Studies: West Africa* (2007).

opinion, and so forth), and individual factors (leaders and their beliefs and motivations).[15]

Therefore, you do know something about these factors (also called "variables"). Now you need

to select an international war. Maybe your professor has lectured on World War I, the 1982

Falklands Island War, and the 1991 Persian Gulf War as examples of international wars.

Learning about the Gulf War piqued your interest in the Middle East region—perhaps you had to

read a bit about U.S.–Iraqi relations and the U.S. invasion of Iraq in 2003 in the context of the

Gulf War and now want to learn more. You have decided that the U.S. invasion of Iraq is the war

on which you'd like to write. So now you have a topic—what next? You have the foundation

(the different factors that can cause war), but now you need to construct the building (examining

the factors—the variables—that might have caused the particular war, in this case the U.S.

invasion). You need to know the parts of the paper and how to organize the paper, and that is

what we turn to next.

Parts of a Research Paper

A research paper is basically composed of three parts: introduction, body, and

conclusion. But those three parts are rather general—a research paper is much more than just

those three, though they are the foundation. Most research papers have the following sections:

Introduction

    Your research question/puzzle

    Road map

    Literature Review

---

[15] In international relations, scholars often use the levels-of-analysis framework that looks at international (systemic), domestic, and individual level factors to explain an event such as the origins of a war. See J. David Singer, "International Conflict: Three Levels of Analysis," *World Politics* 12, 3 (April 1960): 453–61.

Summary of scholarship related to your research question

Thesis/argument based on the existing literature

Research Design

Hypothesis

Methodology

Kinds of sources you will be using

Evidence/Analysis: Testing Your Hypothesis

Discuss and evaluate the evidence

Does the evidence support, or not, your thesis/argument?

Conclusion

Restate the research question, recap your findings

Discuss possible areas of future research

Bibliography or Works-Cited page

List of all the sources used in the paper

Although this is the basic structure of a research paper, you will want to follow your professor's instructions, as she or he might expect a slightly different structure. Using the example of the 2003 U.S. invasion of Iraq, you might need to include a historical background section as part of your introduction or immediately after the research design section. That said, the following briefly describes the main parts of a research paper.

Introduction

The introduction tells the reader what the paper is about, namely, the research question, or puzzle, that you seek to answer. The introduction is an opportunity for the writer to tell the reader why this is an important and interesting research question, or puzzle, for contributing to new knowledge and also builds on previous scholarship on that topic. Besides this being an important question, you want to convey that it is an interesting one too.[16] Why should others be interested in the answer to this research question, let alone the question itself? Finally, you want to select a research question that is doable, or manageable. In other words, a research question that seeks to explain the causes of <u>all</u> civil wars is too big. However, a question that focuses on the causes of one civil war is likely to be feasible.

You will want to end the introduction with your thesis statement. The introduction also provides a "road map," which in essence lays out the parts of the paper.[17] In other words, the road map is providing directions to the reader about the structure of the paper. If you read most introductions to academic journal articles and books, the author provides a road map of what follows (see the box for an example of an introduction with road map). This tells the reader where the paper is going to go. An introduction does not need to be long—but it does need to be clear and concise. You will have seen that there was a road map for the rest of this chapter in the introduction, and there is a road map for the rest of this book in the conclusion of this chapter.

---

[16] Baglione, *Writing a Research Paper in Political Science*, 77.

[17] Many authors refer to the idea of a "road map" for presenting the structure of a paper. See, for example, Baglione, *Writing a Research Paper in Political Science*, 77-78; Amanda McCoy, "Writing a Strong Essay Introduction," March 2, 2010, accessed June 3, 2013, http://suite101.com/article/writing-a-strong-essay-introduction-a208370; Patrick Rael, *Reading, Writing, and Researching for History: A Guide for College Students* (Brunswick, ME: Bowdoin College, 2004), accessed June 3, 2013, http://www.bowdoin.edu/writing-guides/sample%20road%20map.htm.

Maria J. Stephan and Erica Chenoweth, "Why Civil Resistance Works: The Strategic Logic of Nonviolent Conflict," *International Security* 33, 1 (Summer 2008): 7–9.

Implicit in recent scholarly debates about the efficacy of methods of warfare is the assumption that the most effective means of waging political struggle entails violence.[1] Among political scientists, the prevailing view is that opposition movements select violent methods because such means are more effective than nonviolent strategies at achieving policy goals.[2] Despite these assumptions, from 2000 to 2006 organized civilian populations successfully employed nonviolent methods including boycotts, strikes, protests, and organized noncooperation to challenge entrenched power and exact political concessions in Serbia (2000), Madagascar (2002), Georgia (2003) and Ukraine (2004–05), Lebanon (2005), and Nepal (2006).[3] The success of these nonviolent campaigns—especially in light of the enduring violent insurgencies occurring in some of the same countries—begs systematic investigation.

Extant literature provides explanations as to why nonviolent campaigns are effective means of resistance.[4] Little of the literature, however, comprehensively analyzes all known observations of nonviolent and violent insurgencies as analogous resistance types.[5] This study aims to fill this gap by systematically exploring the strategic effectiveness of violent and nonviolent campaigns in conflicts between nonstate and state actors using aggregate data on major nonviolent and violent resistance campaigns from 1900 to 2006.[6] To better understand the causal mechanisms driving these outcomes, we also compare our statistical findings with historical cases that have featured periods of both violent and nonviolent resistance.

Our findings show that major nonviolent campaigns have achieved success 53 percent of the time, compared with 26 percent for violent resistance campaigns.[7]There are two reasons for this success. First, a campaign's commitment to nonviolent methods enhances its domestic and international legitimacy and encourages more broad-based participation in the resistance, which translates into increased pressure being brought to bear on the target. Recognition of the challenge group's grievances can translate into greater internal and external support for that group and alienation of the target regime, undermining the regime's main sources of political, economic, and even military power.

Second, whereas governments easily justify violent counterattacks against armed insurgents, regime violence against nonviolent movements is more likely to backfire against the regime. Potentially sympathetic publics perceive violent militants as having maximalist or extremist goals beyond accommodation, but they perceive nonviolent resistance groups as less extreme, thereby enhancing their appeal and facilitating the extraction of concessions through bargaining.[8]

Our findings challenge the conventional wisdom that violent resistance against conventionally superior adversaries is the most effective way for resistance groups to achieve policy goals. Instead, we assert that nonviolent resistance is a forceful alternative to political violence that can pose effective challenges to democratic and nondemocratic opponents, and at times can do so more effectively than violent resistance.

The article proceeds as follows. The first section presents our main argument. The second section introduces the data set and reports our preliminary empirical findings. In the third section, we evaluate three case studies of nonviolent and violent campaigns in Southeast Asia. We conclude with some theoretical and policy recommendations derived from these findings.

1. Robert A. Pape, *Dying to Win: The Strategic Logic of Suicide Terror* (New York: Random House, 2005); Robert A. Pape, *Bombing to Win: Air Power and Coercion in War* (Ithaca, N.Y.: Cornell University Press, 1996); Daniel L. Byman and Matthew C. Waxman, "Kosovo and the Great Air Power Debate," *International Security*, Vol. 24, No. 4 (Spring 2000), pp. 5–38; Daniel L. Byman, Matthew C. Waxman, and Eric V. Larson, *Air Power as a Coercive Instrument* (Washington, D.C.: RAND, 1999); Daniel Byman and Matthew Waxman, *The Dynamics of Coercion: American Foreign Policy and the Limits of Military Might* (New York: Cambridge University Press, 2002); Michael Horowitz and Dan Reiter, "When Does Aerial Bombing Work? Quantitative Empirical Tests, 1917–1999," *Journal of Conflict Resolution*, Vol. 45, No. 2 (April 2001), pp. 147–173; Max Abrahms, "Why Terrorism Does Not Work," *International Security*, Vol. 31, No. 2 (Fall 2006), pp. 42–78; Gary Clyde Hufbauer, Jeffrey J. Schott, and Kimberly Ann Elliott, *Economic Sanctions Reconsidered: History and Current Policy* (Washington, D.C.: Institute of International Economics, 1992); Robert A. Pape, "Why Economic Sanctions Do Not Work," *International Security*, Vol. 22, No. 2 (Fall 1997), pp. 90–136; Lisa L. Martin, *Coercive Cooperation: Explaining Multilateral Sanctions* (Princeton, N.J.: Princeton University Press, 1992); Jaleh Dashti-Gibson, Patricia Davis, and Benjamin Radcliff, "On the Determinants of the Success of Economic Sanctions: An Empirical Analysis," *American Journal of Political Science*, Vol. 41, No. 2 (April 1997), pp. 608–618; A. Cooper Drury, "Revisiting Economic Sanctions Reconsidered," *Journal of Peace Research*, Vol. 35, No. 4 (July 1998), pp. 497–509; Ivan Arreguín-Toft, *How the Weak Win Wars: A Theory of Asymmetric Conflict* (New York: Cambridge University Press, 2005); Gil Merom, *How Democracies Lose Small Wars: State, Society, and Failures of France in Algeria, Israel in Lebanon, and the United States in Vietnam* (New York: Cambridge University Press, 2003); and Donald Stoker, "Insurgencies Rarely Win—And Iraq Won't Be Any Different (Maybe)," *Foreign Policy*, No. 158 (January/February 2007).
2. See Pape, *Dying to Win*; and Arreguín-Toft, *How the Weak Win Wars*.
3. Robert L. Helvey defines nonviolent methods as "the specific means of action within the technique of nonviolent action" including protest and persuasion, noncooperation, and intervention. See Helvey, *On Strategic Nonviolent Conflict: Thinking about the Fundamentals* (Boston: Albert Einstein Institution, 2004), p. 147.
4. Gene Sharp, *The Politics of Nonviolent Action*, 3 vols. (Boston: Porter Sargent, 1973); Peter Ackerman and Christopher Kruegler, *Strategic Nonviolent Conflict: The Dynamics of People Power in the Twentieth Century* (Westport, Conn.: Praeger, 1994); Adrian Karatnycky and Peter Ackerman, *How Freedom Is Won: From Civic Resistance to Durable Democracy* (Washington, D.C.: Freedom House, 2005); Kurt Schock, *Unarmed Insurrections: People Power Movements in Nondemocracies* (Minneapolis: University of Minnesota Press, 2005); Paul Wehr, Heidi Burgess, and Guy Burgess, eds., *Justice without Violence* (Boulder, Colo.: Lynne Rienner, 1994); Stephen Zunes, "Unarmed Insurrections against Authoritarian Governments in the Third World: A New Kind of Revolution," *Third World Quarterly*, Vol. 15, No. 3 (September 1994), pp. 403–426; Stephen Zunes, Lester Kurtz, and Sarah Beth Asher, eds., *Nonviolent Social Movements: A Geographical Perspective* (Malden, Mass.: Blackwell, 1999); and Vincent Boudreau, *Resisting Dictatorship: Repression and Protest in Southeast Asia* (New York: Cambridge University Press, 2004).
5. A notable exception is Karatnycky and Ackerman, *How Freedom Is Won*.
6. Our use of "resistance" designates major nonstate rebellions, either armed or unarmed. Instead of using event count data, we identify campaigns—a series of repetitive, durable, organized, and observable events directed at a certain target to achieve a goal—as the main unit of analysis. We measure "effectiveness" by comparing stated group objectives to policy outcomes (e.g., states' willingness to make concessions to opposition movements). This analytical distinction is imperfect, but others have used it with success. See Abrahms, "Why Terrorism Does Not Work."
7. Terrorist groups have fared much worse. See ibid., p. 42; and Stoker, "Insurgencies Rarely Win." Our study does not explicitly compare terrorism to nonviolent resistance, but our argument sheds light on why terrorism has been so unsuccessful.

Literature Review

A literature review refers to the body of scholarship on a particular topic. As stated by Jeffrey W. Knopf and Iain McMenamin:

A literature review summarizes and evaluates a body of writings about a specific topic. . . In general, a literature review has two key elements. First, it concisely summarizes the findings or claims that have emerged from prior research efforts on a subject. Second, it reaches a conclusion about how accurate and complete that knowledge is; a literature review presents considered judgments about what's right, what's wrong, what's inconclusive, and what's missing in the existing literature.[18]

In essence, in summarizing and evaluating the existing "state of knowledge" on your research topic, it is also important "to describe the literature in terms of what the existing works have in common, disagree about, and overlook or ignore."[19] An overview of scholarly works, the literature review, matters for understanding what theories are currently applied to a particular topic as well as the evidence that is used to test those theories.

A literature review, therefore, is not a list of authors but rather a presentation of different approaches or theories to a particular topic/research question (see the box below with an example

[18] Jeffrey W. Knopf and Iain McMenamin, "How to Write a Literature Review," in *Publishing Political Science: APSA Guide to Writing and Publishing*, ed. Stephen Yoder (Washington, DC: American Political Science Association, 2008), 101.
[19] Knopf and McMenamin, "How to Write a Literature Review," 113.

of a literature review from the same article with introduction and road map). There are authors who are connected to a particular approach, though. For example, Kenneth Waltz is known as one of the founders of "neo-realism," or "structural realism," in the field of international relations. Even so, when writing about structural realism as an approach to understanding international relations, a literature review would cite Waltz, of course, but also other structural realists, such as Joseph Grieco, John Mearsheimer, and Stephen Walt.[20] In discussing realism in your literature review, you would want to make sure to contrast neo-, or structural, realism with classical realism, as well as neoclassical realism. You also might want to discuss the difference between offensive realism and defensive realism. Thus, it is not the authors that are the focus per se, but the approaches and theories. In the literature review you will discuss the arguments and assumptions of each approach/theory.

The key is figuring out which literature to read and review. This is also related to figuring out what kinds of sources will be good for your project (the process of gathering and evaluating sources will be discussed more fully in Chapter 2). The point is that by writing the literature review, and thus summarizing the existing state of the scholarship on your particular topic, you also are linking this literature to your research topic. In this way, you are demonstrating that you are making a contribution to the literature and building on the research of others.

Having covered the literature as related to your topic, you need to have a thesis, or an argument that you are putting forth that answers your research question. A thesis, according to Gregory M. Scott and Stephen M. Garrison, is "an assertion worth discussing, an argument with more than one possible conclusion. Your thesis sentence will reveal to your reader not only the

---

[20] Steven L. Spiegel, Elizabeth G. Matthews, Jennifer M. Taw, and Kristen P. Williams, *World Politics in a New Era*, 5th ed. (New York: Oxford University Press, 2012), 39. See Joseph Grieco, *Cooperation Among Nations: Europe, America, and Non-Tariff Barriers to Trade* (Ithaca, NY: Cornell University Press, 1990); John J. Mearsheimer, "The False Promise of International Institutions," *International Security* 19, 3 (Winter 1994/1995): 5–49; Walt, *The Origins of Alliances*; and Waltz, *Theories of International Relations*.

argument you have chosen but also your orientation toward it and the conclusion that your paper will attempt to prove."[21] For example, using the case of the U.S. invasion of Iraq, you might have a thesis statement like this:

> The threat from Iraq's weapons of mass destruction led to the U.S. decision to invade Iraq in early 2003.

Maria J. Stephan and Erica Chenoweth, "Why Civil Resistance Works: The Strategic Logic of Nonviolent Conflict," *International Security* 33, 1 (Summer 2008), pp. 9–14.

What Works? The Strategic Logic of Nonviolent Resistance

Nonviolent resistance is a civilian-based method used to wage conflict through social, psychological, economic, and political means without the threat or use of violence. It includes acts of omission, acts of commission, or a combination of both.[9] Scholars have identified hundreds of nonviolent methods—including symbolic protests, economic boycotts, labor strikes, political and social noncooperation, and nonviolent intervention—that groups have used to mobilize publics to oppose or support different policies, to delegitimize adversaries, and to remove or restrict adversaries' sources of power.[10] Nonviolent struggle takes place outside traditional political channels, making it distinct from other nonviolent political processes such as lobbying, electioneering, and legislating.

Strategic nonviolent resistance can be distinguished from principled nonviolence, which is grounded in religious and ethically based injunctions against violence. Although many people who are committed to principled nonviolence have engaged in nonviolent resistance (e.g., Gandhi and Martin Luther King Jr.), the vast majority of participants in nonviolent struggles have not been devoted to principled nonviolence.[11] The conflation of nonviolent struggle with principled nonviolence, pacifism, passivity, weakness, or isolated street protests has contributed to misconceptions about this phenomenon.[12]

Although nonviolent resistors eschew the threat or use of violence, the "peaceful" designation often given to nonviolent movements belies the often highly disruptive nature of organized nonviolent resistance. Nonviolent resistance achieves demands against the will of the opponent by seizing control of the conflict through widespread noncooperation and defiance.[13] Violent coercion threatens physical violence against the opponent.[14]

---

[21] Scott and Garrison, *The Political Science Student Writer's Manual,* 13.

Scholars often assume that violent methods of resistance are the most coercive or the most likely to force accommodation, thereby producing desired policy changes.[15] For instance, some have argued that terrorism is an effective strategy, particularly in forcing democratic regimes to make territorial concessions.[16] In contrast, Max Abrahms has shown that terrorists' success rates are extremely low, accomplishing their policy objectives only 7 percent of the time.[17] Abrahms nevertheless concludes that actors choose terrorism because it is still more effective than nonviolent resistance.[18]

We argue that nonviolent resistance may have a strategic advantage over violent resistance for two reasons. First, repressing nonviolent campaigns may backfire. In backfire, an unjust act—often violent repression—recoils against its originators, often resulting in the breakdown of obedience among regime supporters, mobilization of the population against the regime, and international condemnation of the regime.[19] The internal and external costs of repressing nonviolent campaigns are thus higher than the costs of repressing violent campaigns. Backfire leads to power shifts by increasing the internal solidarity of the resistance campaign, creating dissent and conflicts among the opponent's supporters, increasing external support for the resistance campaign, and decreasing external support for the opponent. These dynamics are more likely to occur when an opponent's violence is not met with violent counterreprisals by the resistance campaign and when this is communicated to internal and external audiences.[20] The domestic and international repercussions of a violent crackdown against civilians who have publicized their commitment to nonviolent action are more severe than repression against those who could be credibly labeled as "terrorists" or "violent insurgents."[21]

Internally, members of a regime—including civil servants, security forces, and members of the judiciary—are more likely to shift loyalty toward nonviolent opposition groups than toward violent opposition groups. The coercive power of any resistance campaign is enhanced by its tendency to prompt disobedience and defections by members of the opponent's security forces, who are more likely to consider the negative political and personal consequences of using repressive violence against unarmed demonstrators than against armed insurgents.[22] Divisions are more likely to result among erstwhile regime supporters, who are not as prepared to deal with mass civil resistance as they are with armed insurgents.[23] Regime repression can also backfire through increased public mobilization. Actively involving a relatively larger number of people in the nonviolent campaign may bring greater and more sustained pressure to bear on the target, whereas the public may eschew violent insurgencies because of physical or moral barriers.

Externally, the international community is more likely to denounce and sanction states for repressing nonviolent campaigns than it is violent campaigns. When nongovernmental organizations (NGOs) sympathize with the cause, nonviolent campaigns are more appealing as aid recipients. External aid may or may not advance the cause of the campaign.[24] The external costs of repressing nonviolent campaigns can be high, however, especially when the repression is captured by the media. External actors may organize sanctions against repressive regimes that repeatedly crack down on unarmed protestors.[25] Although sanctions are possible in the case of violent insurgencies as well, they are less likely. Instead, some foreign states may actually aid a regime in crushing the violent insurgents. Other foreign states may lend material support to a violent resistance campaign in an attempt to advantage it against its opponent. Indeed, state sponsorship of violent insurgencies and terrorist groups has been an ongoing foreign policy dilemma for decades.[26] Whether state-sponsored violent groups have succeeded in obtaining their strategic goals is unclear.

Second, nonviolent resistance campaigns appear to be more open to negotiation and bargaining because they do not threaten the lives or well-being of members of the target regime. Regime supporters are more likely to bargain with resistance groups that are not killing or maiming their comrades.

Correspondence inference theory suggests why nonviolent campaigns may be more appealing to the mass public and more persuasive to regime supporters. The theory posits that a person makes judgments about how to respond to an adversary based on the adversary's actions, which advantages nonviolent resistance in two ways.[27] First, public support is crucial to any resistance, but publics view nonviolent campaigns as physically nonthreatening and violent campaigns as threatening.[28] Nonviolent campaigns appear more amenable to negotiation than violent campaigns, regardless of how disruptive they are. In the face of regime repression, the public is less likely to support a violent campaign that is equally repressive or, at best, careless about civilian casualties. Given a credible alternative, the public is more likely to support a nonviolent campaign.[29]

Second, when violent insurgents threaten the lives of regime members and security forces, they greatly reduce the possibility of loyalty shifts. Abrahms finds that terrorist groups targeting civilians lose public support compared with groups that limit their targets to the military or police.[30] Surrendering or defecting to a violent movement involves greater risk, because the group could kill or torture members of the regime and the regime could violently punish deserters. Because explicitly nonviolent methods do not physically threaten members of the security forces or a regime's civil servants, members of the regime are more likely to shift loyalties toward nonviolent movements rather than toward violent ones. When the regime can no longer rely on the continued cooperation of its security forces or other groups crucial to its control, its grip on power is undermined.

Of course, regime repression of violent insurgencies may backfire as well. Cruel treatment by British military forces in Northern Ireland provided a long-term strategic benefit to the Provisional Irish Republican Army by increasing the number of its supporters. We argue, however, that backfire against violent campaigns is rarer, and that despite temporary setbacks, nonviolent campaigns are more likely to gain additional long-term benefits from regime repression than are violent campaigns.

The aggregate total of the internal and external costs of continued repression may force a regime to accommodate nonviolent campaigns more often than violent ones. The next section tests these assertions.

9. Gene Sharp, ed., *Waging Nonviolent Struggle: 20th Century Practice and 21st Century Potential* (Boston: Porter Sargent, 2005), pp. 41, 547.
10. See Sharp, *The Politics of Nonviolent Action*, vol. 2, in which Sharp lists 198 methods of nonviolent action and gives historical examples of each method.

11. George Lakey, ed., *Powerful Peacemaking: A Strategy for a Living Revolution* (Philadelphia, Pa.: New Society, 1987), p. 87. See also Doug Bond, "Nonviolent Direct Action and Power," in Wehr, Burgess, and Burgess, *Justice without Violence*.

12. Sharp, *The Politics of Nonviolent Action*, 3 vols.; Ackerman and Kruegler, *Strategic Nonviolent Conflict; and Schock, Unarmed Insurrections*.

13. Sharp, *The Politics of Nonviolent Action*, 3 vols. The maintenance of a disciplined, deliberate campaign involves significant collective-action problems, which are the subjects of other studies. See Weinstein, *Inside Rebellion*; and Elisabeth Jean Wood, *Insurgent Collective Action and Civil War in El Salvador* (New York: Cambridge University Press, 2003).

14. Byman and Waxman, *The Dynamics of Coercion*, pp. 30, 50.

15. Pape, *Bombing to Win*; Pape, "Why Economic Sanctions Do Not Work"; and Horowitz and Reiter, "When Does Aerial Bombing Work?"

16. Pape, *Dying to Win*; Ehud Sprinzak; "Rational Fanatics," *Foreign Policy*, No. 120 (September/October 2000), pp. 66–73; David A. Lake, "Rational Extremism: Understanding Terrorism in the Twenty-first Century," *Dialogue-IO*, Vol. 1, No. 1 (Spring 2002), pp. 15–29; Andrew H. Kydd and Barbara F. Walter, "The Strategies of Terrorism," *International Security*, Vol. 31, No. 1 (Fall 2006), pp. 49–80; and Alan M. Dershowitz, *Why Terrorism Works: Understanding the Threat, Responding to the Challenge* (New Haven, Conn.: Yale University Press, 2002).

17. Abrahms, "Why Terrorism Does Not Work," p. 42.

18. Ibid., pp. 41–42.

19. "Moral jiu-jitsu," "political jiu-jitsu," and "backfire" are related but distinct concepts. See Richard B. Gregg, *The Power of Nonviolence*, 2d ed. (New York: Schocken, 1935), pp. 43–65; Sharp, *The Politics of Nonviolent Action*, p. 657; and Brian Martin, *Justice Ignited: The Dynamics of Backfire* (Lanham, Md.: Rowman and Littlefield, 2007), p. 3.

20. Anders Boserup and Andrew Mack, *War without Weapons: Nonviolence in National Defence* (London: Frances Pinter, 1974), p. 84. Other scholars have noted that a combination of sustained confrontation with the opponent, the maintenance of nonviolent discipline, and the existence of a sympathetic audience are necessary conditions to trigger ju-jitsu. See Brian Martin and Wendy Varney, "Nonviolence and Communication," *Journal of Peace Research*, Vol. 40, No. 2 (March 2003), pp. 213–232; and Martin, *Justice Ignited*. Martin qualifies the effects of backfire by emphasizing the importance of media coverage of security forces engaging unarmed protestors. Furthermore, regimes have developed their own strategies to inhibit outrage, thereby limiting the impact of backfire or preventing its emergence entirely.

21. Anika Locke Binnendijk and Ivan Marovic, "Power and Persuasion: Nonviolent Strategies to Influence State Security Forces in Serbia (2000) and Ukraine (2004)," *Communist and Post-Communist Studies*, Vol. 39, No. 3 (September 2006), p. 416.

22. Defections are the withdrawal of support from the incumbent regime. Security forces and civil servants are defecting, for example, when they stop obeying orders and defect from their positions in the state.

23. See Zunes, "Unarmed Insurrections against Authoritarian Governments in the Third World"; Ralph Summy, "Nonviolence and the Case of the Extremely Ruthless Opponent," *Pacifica Review*, Vol. 6, No. 1 (May 1994), pp. 1–29; and Lakey, *Powerful Peacemaking*.

24. External aid may harm the campaign, but this can be true for violent or nonviolent campaigns. See Clifford Bob, *The Marketing of Rebellion: Insurgents, Media, and International Activism* (New York: Cambridge University Press, 2005).

25. We use the list of sanctions identified in Hufbauer, Scott, and Elliott, *Economic Sanctions Reconsidered*.

26. Daniel Byman, *Deadly Connections: States That Sponsor Terrorism* (New York: Cambridge University Press, 2005). See also Jeffrey Record, "External Assistance: Enabler of Insurgent Success," *Parameters*, Vol. 36, No. 3 (Autumn 2006), pp. 36–49.

27. Abrahms, "Why Terrorism Does Not Work."

28. James DeNardo, *Power in Numbers: The Political Strategy of Protest and Rebellion* (Princeton, N.J.: Princeton University Press, 1985).

29. This argument may depend on the "social distance" between resistance movements and their opponents, as social, cultural, religious, and linguistic differences between them could reduce the resistance group's leverage. See Johan Galtung, *Nonviolence in Israel/Palestine* (Honolulu: University of Hawaii Press, 1989), p. 19.

30. Abrahms, "Why Terrorism Does Not Work."

Research Design (Methodology)

Undergraduate political science papers often use cases to answer a research question. As Laura Roselle and Sharon Spray note, a case refers to "an event, issue, policy, or circumstance that you will study." This is also known as the case-study approach: "[a] case-based research approach is based on the systematic gathering and comparison of evidence in one or more cases to answer a narrowly defined question."[22] By looking at one case in depth or comparing more than one case, you will formulate a hypothesis (or hypotheses) and determine which variables, or factors, you will be using to answer your research question. Thus, the research design section includes two main parts: your hypothesis and the variables. The variables are what you will be measuring (also called "operationalizing") and comparing when trying to answer your research question and test your hypothesis.[23]

So how do you go about constructing a hypothesis? As James M. Carlson and Mark S. Hyde note, "the formulation of hypotheses guides research and provides focus. . . . A well-constructed hypothesis provides guidance for data collection and analysis. Ultimately, the quality of the hypothesis influences the ease with which research is conducted and the inferences that can be made about the predictability and accuracy of theory."[24] A hypothesis, as defined by Lisa Baglione, "is your 'best guess' about the links between the independent and dependent variables. Of course, it is an educated guess, as you have surveyed the scholarly work on this question and

---

[22] Roselle and Spray, *Research and Writing in International Relations*, 35.
[23] Roselle and Spray, *Research and Writing in International Relations*, 36, 62–63.
[24] Carlson and Hyde, *Doing Empirical Political Research*, 59.

assessed its logic in your literature review."[25] Importantly, in constructing a hypothesis, you need

to have a hypothesis that can be tested by using empirical evidence.[26]

The independent (also called an "explanatory") variable refers to "a causal factor; that

which acts on something else." The dependent variable refers to "that which is acted upon."[27] In

thinking about the relationship between the independent variables and the dependent variable

you are looking for correlation or causation. A correlation is "[a] relationship between two

variables."[28] Causation refers to "the relationship of cause and effect."[29] Did the independent

variable(s) cause the dependent variable? If you were interested in examining a possible gender

gap in voting behavior in U.S. presidential elections, your research question might be: What role

does gender play in people's votes for U.S. presidential candidates? The dependent variable

would be presidential voting choices. This is where the literature review informs your research

design and demonstrates the utility of scholarly works for theory and evidence as applied to your

research topic. Having surveyed the scholarly literature on the gender gap in voting behavior,

you will find that there are several variables, or factors, that could explain individuals' voting

choices (correlation or causation). For example, one independent variable would be gender.

Other independent variables could be race, party identification (or preference), age, and marital

status. You might also need to consider income, participation in the labor force, religion,

ethnicity, and education level as additional variables that could influence the voting choices of

men and women.[30]

---

[25] Baglione, *Writing a Research Paper in Political Science*, 66.

[26] Carlson and Hyde, *Doing Empirical Political Research*, 60.

[27] Spiegel et al., *World Politics in a New Era*, 30. For more on research design in political science, see Van Evera, *Guide to Methods for Students of Political Science*, chapter 1.

[28] Spiegel, et al., *World Politics in a New Era*, 28.

[29] Spiegel, et al., *World Politics in a New Era*, 30.

[30] Gender and presidential vote exercise from Sharon Krefetz's Political Science Research Methods course, Clark University (Fall 2012). For more on the gender gap, see also Karen M. Kaufmann, "The Gender Gap," *PS: Political Science and Politics* (July 2006): 447–53.

In constructing your hypotheses for the question of the role of gender in an individual's voting choice in presidential elections, you might consider the following:

H1: Women are more likely than men to vote for Democratic presidential candidates.

In this research design/methodology section, you will also want to inform the reader of the types of sources you used for your research, such as polls, surveys, interviews, journal articles, and books. Using our example of gender and presidential vote, you might want to consult exit polls of voters' candidate choices in presidential elections over the last several election cycles. You would also look to existing scholarship in books and journal articles related to your research question.

Evidence/Analysis: Testing Your Hypothesis

This section is focused on presenting the evidence you have accumulated about your research question. Political scientists use two means of analysis: quantitative and qualitative research. In using a quantitative analysis, the researcher is using numerical data, or information, whereas in using qualitative analysis, the researcher "assesses evidence or facts in the form of words to determine where the weight of it lies—on the side of the thesis or against it."[31]

Political science undergraduate courses tend to focus on qualitative analysis (although research methods courses, sometimes required of political science majors, cover quantitative and qualitative analyses and probably would require students to complete assignments using both kinds of analyses). For example, in studying realism and liberalism to explain international relations topics, students are exposed to qualitative analysis. In this way, the strength and

---

[31] Baglione, *Writing a Research Paper in Political Science*, 118.

weaknesses of the arguments and assumptions of the theories are made and compared to come to

a conclusion about which theory might best explain a particular topic being studied. If you were

to look at United Nations Security Council Resolution 1441, passed unanimously in late 2002,

which called for Iraq to comply with the disarmament provisions specified in earlier resolutions,

how would realist and liberal explanations account for the decision? Was it because of Iraq's

perceived threat to the security and stability of the international system and the regional balance

of power (realist explanation)? Was it because of the effectiveness of international institutions in

responding to threats to international security (liberal explanation)? What are the strengths and

weakness of the realist and liberal explanations in explaining the UN Security Council's

decision? Which theory is most convincing to you based on the evidence?

Although most political science research papers use qualitative analysis, some require the

use of quantitative analysis. Such projects use statistical analysis for large-n studies (large-n just

refers to a large number of cases to study the relationship between the independent and

dependent variables). Using our example of gender and U.S. presidential vote, you might look to

organizations that conduct polls of registered voters on election day. The Gallup Poll, for

example, covers all elections since 1952 to show the difference in voting between men and

women.[32] The Center for American Women and Politics at Rutgers University also provides data

on gender and women's participation, including voter turnout. The American National Election

Studies (ANES) conducts surveys that provide data on political participation, public opinion, and

voting.[33] In using these data, scholars then use statistical software packages (such as SPSS and

---

[32] Jeffrey M. Jones, "Gender Gap in 2012 Vote Is Largest in Gallup's History," November 9, 2012, http://www.gallup.com/poll/158588/gender-gap-2012-vote-largest-gallup-history.aspx?.
[33] Center for American Women and Politics, http://www.cawp.rutgers.edu/; American National Election Studies, http://www.electionstudies.org/.

Stata) to run statistical analyses of the relationship between the independent and dependent variables.

Regardless of whether you use qualitative or quantitative analyses (or both) in your papers, in presenting your findings you are in essence answering the question: How do I know? In this section, you are making your case for your hypothesis and thesis. You are testing your hypothesis by using the empirical evidence you have gathered and weighing that evidence to determine whether your hypothesis is correct.

Conclusion

The conclusion is where you restate the research question, or puzzle. But you do more than just that. A conclusion really is a wrap-up of the entire paper—you recap the scholarly literature you addressed as well as your findings. You can also discuss whether your findings are generalizable. In other words, are they "applicable to other situations, issues, and cases"?[34] Can your results be applied to other cases? For example, if your thesis about the U.S. invasion of Iraq was that realist theory best explains the decision to invade, can realism be used to explain other cases in which the United States decided to invade another country (e.g., Panama in 1989, Afghanistan in 2001)? If your paper examined the factors that led to the outbreak of the Russian Revolution, can the same factors be used to explain the outbreak of other revolutions? If your paper examined the factors that led to the transition to democracy in Latin America, do the same factors account for the transition to democracy in Eastern Europe?

---

[34] Spiegel et al., *World Politics in a New Era*, 35.

Bibliography or works cited page

The last piece of a research paper is the bibliography, also called a references list or works-cited list. The formatting of the bibliography differs depending on which citation style is used (see Chapter 4 for these different styles). The bibliography lists all the sources used in the paper, in alphabetical order by author's last name. A bibliography allows the reader to know where you got the information used in the paper—and whether those sources are credible. The reader can then go to those sources if she or he is interested in the topic.

CONCLUSION

Just as it was mentioned that a research paper has a road map, so too does this chapter. The road map tells you, the reader, what the rest of the book will cover, so you now know what follows. Chapter 2, "Conducting Research," discusses the research process itself. The chapter covers the importance of good note taking and organizing the research and discusses the differences between types of sources (primary, secondary, tertiary), books, journals, periodicals, and the Internet. It also includes an overview of databases that are particularly useful for political science research projects.

As the first two chapters focus on the structure of a research paper and the research process, Chapter 3 is focused on the writing process itself. The essence of good writing is to write, rewrite, revise, and edit. This chapter also provides information on formatting a paper (pagination, font size, use of headings, etc.). Writing a research paper involves documenting the research—and that means citations. Chapter 4, "Citations and Bibliography," familiarizes students with the different citation styles that scholars use and that professors expect their

students to use in their research papers. Chapter 5 provides a brief conclusion to the guide and a

short list of very good sources for further readings on writing research papers in general and

political science papers specifically.

Chapter 2

Conducting Research: Finding, Evaluating, and Using Sources

Chapter 1 provided you with the basic structure of a research paper. Now you have to get started doing the actual research as you go about writing the literature review section. The question is how and where to begin. Scholars begin the research process by finding information and evaluating that information. Where do they look? What kinds of sources do they look for in their research process? How does technology aid scholars in the research process? How do scholars judge that the sources of information are of good quality and are credible? This chapter begins with an overview of the research process, namely, finding, evaluating, and using sources—what scholars consider when they begin the research process in order to answer the research question. There are several subsections on the types of sources scholars use, including differentiating primary and secondary sources, as well as books, academic journals, and newspapers and magazines. The most frequently used databases will be addressed, and then a brief discussion of using and evaluating Internet sources follows. Finally, though much research can be done by accessing materials online, the library and librarians are still a very important component of the research process, and their contributions will be discussed in the section that follows. The chapter concludes with suggestions for effective note taking.

SCHOLARLY SOURCES: What are they?

Scholars begin by looking at the research done by other scholars. As Roselle and Spray note, "They do so because the goal is to build knowledge of political phenomena. This is accomplished by establishing links between various research projects, thereby creating an ongoing accumulation of knowledge established one study at a time."[1] This accumulation of

knowledge is usually found in scholarly sources. Such sources are usually those found in peer-

reviewed books and academic journal articles. Peer review (or "refereed") is a process by which

an author submits a book or an article to a publisher for publication. Before the book or article is

accepted for publication, it goes through a review process. The publisher asks experts in a

specific field to review and assess (anonymously) the work to see if it is of high quality and

should be published. Knowing that an article or book has been peer-reviewed gives it more

credibility.

Primary and Secondary Sources

In thinking about the kinds of sources available for research projects, scholars may look

to archival data that includes diaries, letters, government reports, and speeches. They also may

conduct surveys or interviews. All these are considered primary sources—they are the "firsthand

evidence, reported by whoever first produced or collected the data."[2] As original materials,

primary sources "are from the time period involved and have not been filtered through

interpretation or evaluation. Primary sources are original materials on which other research is

based."[3] In the box below is an example of a primary document. In October 1962, the United

States discovered that the Soviets had placed medium-range nuclear weapons in Cuba. The

United States wanted the Soviets to withdraw the missiles, and that led to an event known as the

---

[1] Laura Roselle and Sharon Spray, *Research and Writing in International Relations* (New York: Pearson Longman, 2008), 17.

[2] Kate L. Turabian, *Student's Guide to Writing College Papers*, 4th ed., revised by Gregory G. Colomb, Joseph M. Williams, and the University of Chicago Press Editorial Staff (Chicago: University of Chicago Press, 2010), 45.

[3] University of Maryland, University Libraries, "Primary, Secondary and Tertiary Sources," accessed May 31, 2011, http://www.lib.umd.edu/guides/primary-sources.html.

Cuban Missile Crisis. The primary document is a nonclassified document of talking points:

"Reasons Against Concentrating on Soviets."

Sample of a Primary Source: Non-Classified, Talking Points, "Reasons Against Concentrating on Soviets," October 16, 1962; Digital National Security Archive, item: CC00682; http://nsarchive.chadwyck.com/nsa/documents/CC/00682/all.pdf

<u>Talking Points</u> :   Reasons Against Concentrating on Soviets.

1. Soviets themselves have carefully avoided mentioning their presence.

2. Soviets consistently blur US missile programs in other countries by suggesting we are turning missiles over to host country. Just this evening TASS put out story US was truning Jupiters over to Turks, training them in use of missiles.

3. Exclusive fix on Soviets permits them only two basic choices: call off the program or fight to maintain it. We believe they ultimately would not risk World War III <u>but</u>, Soviets will almost certainly <u>act as</u> though they would risk it and we will have extremely difficult time assessing their intentions.

4. <u>Consequently</u>, by narrowing Soviet choices while putting them under pressure to give appearance of not backing down possibilities of miscalculation and escalation will be increased.

5. <u>Moreover</u>, as direct US-Soviet confrontation mounts, original reason for US action will become obscure and world (as well as domestic opinion) will focus on then developing crisis. Pressures on US to cease and desist will rise and in this situation various deals involving US deployments abroad will be increasingly advocated.

6. By concentrating on Cubans (or at least leaving some doubt about who we are concentrating on) we merely do what Soviets have been doing to our allies with some success for years (Iran, Scandinavia);

7. We permit Soviets opportunity to maneuver in situation where US-Soviet confrontation is not yet direct.

8. We permit Soviet opportunity to back off even though proclaiming their undying fidelity to Castro.

9. Soviet and other peoples offers for deals of one sort or another can be confronted more calmly because US-Soviet military confrontation will not yet have developed to grave crisis point.

10. Castro already has image of intemperance; Castro with missiles is easire target for us than USSR. (In UN for example)

11.

RH PLEASE NOTE: If you win battle one, limited blockade clearly involving only Soviet ships becomes a contradiction. Hence I believe it is almost inevitable that <u>both</u> battles must be fought simultaneously. Clearly those who opted for least immediately risky course (limited blockade) realized that it makes sense only if main explicit enemy is Soviet.

Secondary sources, which are "created by someone without firsthand experience," also are used by scholars.[4] Secondary sources include books and academic articles about particular topics that the researcher is interested in evaluating and analyzing.[5] Secondary sources "are interpretations and evaluations of primary sources . . . [they] are not evidence, but rather commentary on and discussion of evidence."[6] Using the primary source example above, the secondary source would be a work that discussed the document "Reasons Against Concentrating on Soviets" in the context of U.S. foreign policy.

Academic research is a combination of primary and secondary sources. Scholars may conduct a survey and interpret its results. They also interpret the primary sources of other scholars as part of their literature review and the presentation of their research. They also look to the works of others who have worked with and evaluated secondary sources. All of this contributes to increasing the body of knowledge.

Books

Books are excellent sources for research because they tend to be in-depth analyses of topics and subject areas, providing multiple case studies. As Will Sherman writes, "the book provides a focused, yet comprehensive study that summarizes years of research by an author—or

---

[4] Library of Congress, "Using Primary Sources," accessed May 31, 2011, http://www.loc.gov/teachers/usingprimarysources/.

[5] Library of Congress, "American Women: The General Collections," accessed May 31, 2011, http://memory.loc.gov/ammem/awhhtml/awgc1/index.html.

[6] Sometimes sources are further divided into tertiary sources, such as those found in encyclopedias and dictionaries, which "consist of information which is a distillation and collection of primary and secondary sources," but those considered tertiary sources are often considered secondary sources too. There doesn't seem to be a hard and fast rule about distinguishing between secondary and tertiary sources. See University of Maryland, University Libraries, "Primary, Secondary and Tertiary Sources," accessed May 31, 2011, http://www.lib.umd.edu/guides/primary-sources.html.

team of authors—who have devoted their academic [work] to a particular subject area."[7] The

citations and bibliographies found at the back of a book are a great way to find further sources

for your paper as they provide a body of literature on a particular topic.

It is also important to keep in mind whether a publisher is a reputable press. In political

science (and other academic disciplines), reputable presses include university presses, such as

Oxford University Press, Harvard University Press, Chicago University Press, and Stanford

University Press, as well "trade" presses, such as Lynne Rienner, Palgrave, Routledge, Rowman

and Littlefield, and Westview, to name a few.

When you are searching for books, most library online computer catalogs allow a search

by "keyword," "title," or "author." Once you have inserted one of these search words, an entry

will be shown on the screen. The entry will include several pieces of information, including the

book's title, the author's name, the location (library stacks), the publisher, the call number, and

the subject. Most online catalog systems will allow the user to click on the author's name, which

will bring up a list other publications by that author. Clicking on the call number will show

books that are in the same call number range, as books are usually cataloged by subject. A

library's online catalog can lead to further sources.

Scholarly journals (includes articles and book reviews)

Although many scholars write books, they also write academic journal articles. These

articles provide literature reviews that present and evaluate the scholarly research on a particular

topic, as well as making their own argument and providing evidence in support of that argument.

Many journal articles are shortened versions of a book, perhaps presenting one case study

---

[7] Will Sherman, "33 Reasons Why Libraries and Librarians Are Still Extremely Important," *Library News*, February 1, 2007, accessed May 14, 2013, http://greatlibrarynews.blogspot.ca/2007/02/33-reasons-why-libraries-and.html.

(whereas a book might have several case studies). Journal articles also provide additional sources through their citations and references. A good way to assess whether a journal article might be of use for your research paper is to read the abstract, which briefly describes what the article is about (see the sample abstract in the box below).

Sample Abstract

Greed, grievances, and mobilization are generally offered as explanations for rebellion and civil war. The authors extend arguments about the precursors to nonviolent protest, violent rebellion, and civil war. These arguments motivate a series of hypotheses that are tested against data from the Minorities at Risk project. The results of the analysis suggest, first, that the factors that predict antistate activity at one level of violence do not always hold at other levels; second, the response by the state has a large impact on the subsequent behavior of the rebels; and third, the popular notion of diamonds fueling civil unrest is generally not supported. The authors draw inferences from their results to future theoretical and policy development.

Patrick M. Regan and Daniel Norton, "Greed, Grievance, and Mobilization in Civil Wars," *Journal of Conflict Resolution* 49, 3 (June 2005): 319.

Book reviews are also found in scholarly journals. A book review is an examination and evaluation of a published work. The reviewer sets out to describe the book (its thesis and theoretical framework), where it fits into the existing and relevant scholarly literature, whether

and how well the book makes a contribution to the literature (whether the book made a

convincing argument, providing evidence in support of that argument), and who the target

audience is that would benefit from reading the book. Reading a book review can help you

determine whether the book itself will be of use to your research paper (see the book review

below).

Sample Book Review

Women's Access to Political Power in Post-Communist Europe. Edited by Richard E. Matland and Kathleen A. Montgomery. Oxford University Press, 2003. 369 p. $85.00 cloth, $35.00 paper.

Valerie Sperling, *Clark University*

It was something of a truism that within the political institutions of the Soviet bloc states, women and power were found in inverse proportion to each other. While women occupied roughly 30% of the seats within the faux-parliamentary bodies of the communist region, true power was never located in those institutions. Instead, political power was found at the communist party's zenith, where women were seen rarely, if at all.

       The collapse of Communist-Party-run dictatorships across Eastern Europe presented scholars with an opportunity to test various political science theories derived largely from the study of western democracies. The editors of this volume are concerned primarily with testing theories of representation. In particular, they seek to explain the causes of women's low representation in postcommunist parliaments. The 18 contributors hail from across Europe and the United States, and present case studies on Germany, Lithuania, Hungary, Ukraine, Russia (including a chapter on regional elections), Macedonia, Poland, the Czech Republic, Slovenia, Croatia, and Bulgaria.

       While the authors do not deny that the postcommunist region features several "legacy" characteristics that could depress women's representation (such as seeing women in parliament as Communist Party-sponsored tokens), they largely agree that the paucity of women in parliaments there stems from institutional sources. These include electoral rules, such as the use of proportional representation (PR) versus a majoritarian system, and party rules, such as the use of quotas. However, the authors do not suggest that institutional rules are the only thing promoting or preventing women's equal representation. They portray women's representation as being determined by supply and demand: Supply is governed by the number of women wishing to run for office, and demand is determined by the voters, on the one hand, and by party "gatekeepers" on the other. Meanwhile, many sociocultural and economic calculations and preconditions factor into the choices made by potential female candidates, party gatekeepers, and voters. Suffice it to say that women's underrepresentation is overdetermined (and not only in postcommunist Europe).

Several findings hold across most of the countries included in this study. First, institutional rules matter for women's level of representation. PR benefits women when the number of seats contested in a given district is high. Parties can then win larger numbers of seats, allowing in candidates beyond the few top slots on the lists. PR thus leads to the presence of more women in parliament than does a single-mandate district system (as is typically true in Western democracies). There are some exceptions to this rule (notably Russia and Hungary). The Russian mixed-system case highlights the fact that PR is not sufficient to promote women's representation. There, party fragmentation works against women's successful election to PR seats, as does the way that party lists are composed (through patronage), whereby women are often placed in "unwinnable spots" (p. 162). In Russia's 1993 election, across all the party lists, "90 percent [of women] were below thirtieth place on the lists" (p. 163).

Another finding consistent across several countries is that women's organizing is crucial in order to improve female representation on party lists. As Frederick Douglass said, "Power concedes nothing without a demand." In the Polish case, a main cause of the increase in the number of women elected between 1997 and 2001 was that women across parties during the election campaign in 2001 supported a "Pre-Electoral Coalition of Women," the purpose of which was to increase the number of female parliamentarians, and which sported slogans like "Enough adoration--we want representation" (p. 232). As a result of such public pressure, combined with efforts by women within the political parties, some parties instituted sex-based quotas.

Sociocultural factors also influence women's representation. The authors of one chapter cite cross-country poll data showing that majorities of men and women in the region believe that men make better political leaders than do women. "Demand" for women in power is thus low. However, as the editors point out, some of the countries there have increased women's representation, despite such attitudes. The data in the case study chapters show that, to some extent, such increases are traceable to the introduction of PR systems, and to the change over time in party predominance, with leftist parties in particular coming to power, bringing more women into parliament with them. The most interesting case of shifting party fortunes giving rise to more women in parliament comes from Bulgaria, where, in 2001, the former king hitched his electoral efforts to a little-known women's party (of necessity, since his own party was refused registration) and won, thereby bringing the percentage of women in the parliament up to 26.7% from a mere 10.4% in the previous election (p. 316).

Other evidence reveals the underlying sexism that leads party gatekeepers to erect high barriers to female candidates' inclusion on party lists. Several chapters note the fact that women must be "hyperqualified" (p. 207) in order to receive a party's nomination; they are often better educated than male members of parliament, and also must "prove" their legitimacy more extensively than men do. In Poland, for example, in 1993, 73% of the women members of parliament had been members of Solidarity in 1980, whereas this was true of only 49% of male MPs (p. 219).

On the whole, this is a highly readable book that tells the reader an impressive amount about politics and women's representation in postcommunist Europe. The first two chapters set out the research questions and theoretical framework. All of the chapters are written in an accessible style, and the project sensibly combines qualitative and quantitative data in order to best make sense of the diverse levels of women's representation in the chosen countries. The case study chapters are densely packed with empirical data. They feature rich detail and complex explanations, exploring the factors laid out in the theoretical framework, such as public opinion, electoral institutions, party rules, and the change over time in the dominance of political parties. *Women's Access to Political Power in Post-Communist Europe* has a high level of coherence, since each of the cases is explored within the same theoretical framework. The chapters are punctuated by useful at-a-glance tables comparing electoral rules, levels of female representation, and so on. Any study of elections and politics in these countries from here on should take these valuable contributions into account. Gender can no longer be ignored in studies of elections in the postcommunist world.

Valerie Sperling review of *Women's Access to Political Power in Post-Communist Europe*, edited by Richard E. Matland and Kathleen A. Montgomery. New York: Oxford University Press, 2003, in *Perspectives on Politics* 2, 4 (December 2004): 878–79.

Finding Scholarly Journal Articles and Book Reviews

There are several online databases in which scholarly articles, book reviews, and newspapers can be found. Some of the most frequently used ones in political science are JSTOR, LexisNexis Academic, PAIS International, Project Muse, Social Sciences Citation Index, Worldwide Political Science Abstracts, and Expanded Academic ASAP. This is by no means an exhaustive list. You should check your university's library website for the databases that you will be able to access from the library homepage.

To give you a sense of what you can find in these databases, JSTOR (Journal Storage) is a database in which "printed scholarly journal" articles in the social sciences and humanities have been digitized: converted into electronic (pdf) files and stored for retrieval by users.[8] The database is divided into 55 disciplines, and within each discipline are the listings of the journals

---

[8] JSTOR, "About: 10 Things," accessed May 15, 2013, http://about.jstor.org/10things.

available (as this is an archive, there is a gap of a few years until a journal volume is available; a current volume and issue should be available in hard copy at your library or through an interlibrary loan). Disciplines covered include African American Studies, Archeology, Art and Art History, Asian Studies, Economics, Education, Jewish Studies, Psychology, and so forth. In the case of Political Science, more than 150 journals are accessible. Some of the major ones of use available on JSTOR include *American Journal of Political Science, American Political Science Review, British Journal of Political Science, Canadian Journal of Political Science, Comparative Politics, Foreign Affairs, International Organization, International Security, International Studies Quarterly, Journal of Conflict Resolution, Journal of Peace Research, Journal of Politics, Legislative Studies Quarterly, Political Psychology, Political Research Quarterly, Presidential Studies Quarterly, Review of International Studies, Third World Quarterly,* and *World Politics*.

There are journals in other disciplines that political scientists also use. For example, under Feminist and Women's Studies, students might want to look at *Gender and Development* or *Journal of Middle East Women's Studies*. Under History, journals such as *The American Historical Review, Contemporary European History, The International History Review, The Journal of Military History*, and the *Journal of World History* might have useful articles for political science papers. The same goes for journals in Latin American Studies (e.g., *Journal of Latin American Studies, Latin American Politics and Society*), Law (e.g., *The American Journal of International Law, Human Rights Quarterly*), Middle East Studies (*International Journal of Middle East Studies, Middle East Report, Journal of Palestine Studies*), and Population Studies (*Journal of Population Economics, International Migration Review, Population and Environment*).

LexisNexis Academic provides access to newspapers and magazines, legal cases in the United States (federal and state going back to 1789), country socioeconomic profiles, public figures, and companies. LexisNexis provides "access [to] over 10,000 news, business, and legal sources . . . [and] includes deep backfiles and up-to-the-minute stories in national and regional newspapers, wire services, broadcast transcripts, international news, and non-English language sources."[9]

PAIS International "contains citations to journal articles, books, government documents, statistical directories, . . . research reports, conference reports, publications of international agencies, . . . Internet material. . . ." Subject areas covered that are related to political science, and to international relations in particular, include economic conditions, energy resources and policy, environment, government, human rights, international relations, military and defense policy, politics, and trade.[10]

Project Muse contains scholarly journal articles in the social sciences (as well as humanities and mathematics).[11] Social Sciences Citation Index provides access to journal articles, and the Worldwide Political Science Abstracts contains books, dissertations, journal articles, and working papers in the area of international relations in political science, including international law, comparative politics, military policy, environmental policy, and public administration/policy.[12] Expanded Academic ASAP and Academic OneFile provide access to

---

[9] LexisNexis Academic, "Product Overview," accessed May 31, 2011, http://academic.lexisnexis.com/online-services/academic/academic-overview.aspx.
[10] PAIS International and PAIS Archives, "Fact Sheets," accessed May 31, 2011, http://www.csa.com/factsheets/pais-set-c.php.
[11] "About Project Muse," http://muse.jhu.edu/.
[12] CSA Worldwide Political Science Abstracts, "Fact Sheets," http://www.csa.com/factsheets/polsci-set-c.php.

peer-reviewed journal articles, reference sources, and periodicals and newspapers in a wide range of disciplines.[13]

As was noted at the outset, these are the primary databases used in the social sciences but by no means the only ones. Again, do check out your library's webpage for the other online sources for journal articles, books, newspapers, and so forth, available for your use.

Newspapers and magazines

Newspapers (such as *The New York Times*, *The Times of London*, *The Boston Globe*, *The Wall Street Journal*, and *The Los Angeles Times*) and magazines (*TIME*, *Newsweek*, *The Atlantic Monthly*, *The Economist*, and so forth) are also good sources for researching political science topics. It is important to keep in mind, however, that they are written for a general audience, whether it is a national or local newspaper or a magazine. Moreover, these publications also may have a particular ideological point of view (liberal? conservative?), of which the researcher should be mindful.[14] Articles in newspapers and magazines can be found in some of the databases noted above, such as LexisNexis Academic.

Data and Statistical Sources

In addition to journal articles and books, scholars use databases and statistical sources when gathering primary evidence such as government documents and polling data. Several to highlight for political science include the Inter-university Consortium for Political and Social Research (ICPSR), the World Bank, and the Eurobarometer, but again, this is not an exhaustive

---

[13] Expanded Academic ASAP, accessed May 27, 2011,
http://www.gale.cengage.com/PeriodicalSolutions/academicAsap.htm?grid=ExpandedAcademicASAPRedirect;
Academic OneFile, accessed May 27, 2011,
http://www.gale.cengage.com/PeriodicalSolutions/academicOnefile.htm.
[14] Baglione, *Writing a Research Paper*, 18.

list. ICPSR, for example, "maintains a data archive of more than 500,000 files of research in the social sciences. It hosts 16 specialized collections of data in education, aging, criminal justice, substance abuse, terrorism, and other fields."[15] The World Bank publishes data on a variety of topics, including development, health, poverty, gender, environment, and social development. The Eurobarometer is the survey of people in the member-states of the European Union on a wide variety of issues, including national identity and support for the EU.[16]

For data specifically related to American politics, you also might want to look at the American National Election Studies (ANES), the U.S. Census Bureau, the Digital National Security Archive, and the U.S. Congressional Serial Set, 1817–1994. Through the University of Michigan, the ANES conducts public opinion surveys every election year, and it is a great resource for studying electoral behavior. The Census Bureau collects an array of data on housing, income, migration, immigration, and poverty, for example. It also conducts research in other countries.[17]

The Digital National Security Archive is a database with more than 80,000 declassified documents related to U.S. foreign policy and national security policy decisions. According to its website, "Each of these collections, compiled by top scholars and experts, exhaustively covers the most critical world events, countries, and U.S. policy decisions from post World War II through the 21st century."[18] The U.S. Congressional Serial Set contains all publications from the 15th through the 96th Congress.[19]

---

[15] Inter-university Consortium for Political and Social Research, "About ICPSR," http://www.icpsr.umich.edu/icpsrweb/content/membership/about.html.
[16] The World Bank, http://www.worldbank.org; European Commission, "Public Opinion," accessed May 14, 2013, http://ec.europa.eu/public_opinion/index_en.htm.
[17] American National Election Studies, www.electionstudies.org; Digital National Security Archive, nsarchive.chadwyck.com/; U.S. Census Bureau, www.census.gov; U.S. Congressional Serial Set, www.gpo.gov/help/u.s._congressional_serial_set.htm.
[18] Digital National Security Archive, *The National Security Archive*, nsarchive.chadwyck.com/marketing/index.jsp.
[19] U.S. Congressional Serial Set, www.gpo.gov/help/u.s._congressional_serial_set.htm.

As with databases for journal articles and book reviews, the databases for statistical analysis are vast and varied. Be sure to check your library's website and talk with your professors about other sources that are relevant to your topic.

Internet

The Internet is a great resource for finding information. What matters is figuring out which kinds of websites are credible and which ones are not. Many students may do a quick Google search, typing in key words related to their topic. Many find Wikipedia a good place to start to familiarize themselves with a particular topic. However, it should not form the basis of your research. In fact, many professors discourage students from using and citing Wikipedia in their research papers because it is not peer-reviewed as is the case with scholarly books and articles. As Harvard University's College Writing Program website states: "As its own disclaimer states, information on Wikipedia is contributed by anyone who wants to post material, and the expertise of the posters is not taken into consideration. Users may be reading information that is outdated or that has been posted by someone who is not an expert in the field or by someone who wishes to provide misinformation. . . . Some information on Wikipedia may well be accurate, but because experts do not review the site's entries, there is a considerable risk in relying on this source for your essays."[20] According to Wikipedia's website, "In general the most reliable sources are peer-reviewed journals and books published in university presses; university-level textbooks; magazines, journals, and books published by respected publishing houses; and mainstream newspapers."[21] That said, Wikipedia does offer basic information that may be of use

---

[20] "What's Wrong with Wikipedia?" Harvard Guide to Using Sources, Harvard College Writing Program, accessed February 25, 2013, http://isites.harvard.edu/icb/icb.do?keyword=k70847&pageid=icb.page346376.
[21] "Wikipedia: No Original Research," accessed February 25, 2013, http://simple.wikipedia.org/wiki/Wikipedia:No_original_research.

to you as you are getting a grasp of the topic at hand. The key is to be able to distinguish academic/scholarly works from others when writing a research paper.

Scholars look at the information found in well-known nongovernmental organizations (NGOs), international governmental organizations (IGOs), and government websites. For example, if you were writing a paper on human rights violations in China, you might want to look at Human Rights Watch (www.hrw.org) or Amnesty International (www.amnesty.org). If you were writing a paper on the international economy, you might want to look at the World Trade Organization (www.wto.org), the World Bank (www.worldbank.org), or the European Union (www.europa.eu). If you were writing on the impact of war on women or on peacekeeping, you might look at the United Nations (www.un.org) or the website for the Women's International League for Peace and Freedom (www.peacewomen.org). If you were writing a paper on U.S. domestic policy and social program issues such as education, health-care insurance, and Social Security, you could consult the Library of Congress's Congressional Research Service website (http://www.loc.gov/crsinfo/) for its reports. Just typing in "human rights," "international economy," "peacekeeping," and "U.S. domestic policy" in the Google or Yahoo search box does not guarantee that you will find reputable sources. You have to know where to look and how to evaluate the source.

You also might want to look at Internet news websites such as CNN (http://www.cnn.com), ABC News (www.abcnews.com), The Economist (www.economist.com), and the British Broadcasting Corporation, or BBC (http://news.bbc.co.uk). There are also many English-language sites for non-English-speaking news sources, such as Al-Jazeera (http://english.aljazeera.net). These are good starting points, particularly for up-to-date coverage of current events. They provide quotes from government officials, conduct public opinion polls and other surveys, and offer in-depth reporting on various political issues.

UCLA's College Library's "Thinking Critically about World Wide Web Resources" provides a list of questions to be asked when evaluating an internet source, such as the following:

- Who is the audience?

- How complete and accurate are the information and the links provided?

- Does the site claim to represent a group, an organization, an institution, a corporation or a governmental body?

- Is advertising included at the site, and if so, has it had an impact on the content?

- Who is the author or sponsor?

- What is the authority or expertise of the individual or group that created this site?

- Is any sort of bias evident?[22]

In essence, it is vitally important to be a savvy consumer of information found on the Internet. If in doubt, ask your professor. Do not assume that because the information you found on the Internet is there, it must be true.

Library and the librarians

This chapter on finding and evaluating sources would not be complete without a brief section on the library and librarians. Libraries and librarians remain important resources for research. Although it is easy to get caught up in the immediacy and ease of using the Internet, the

---

[22] "Thinking Critically about World Wide Web Resources," created by Esther Grassian, the UCLA Library, and used with permission, June 1995, accessed May 11, 2011, http://www2.library.ucla.edu/libraries/college/11605_12337.cfm.

physical space of a library houses books that are not available for downloading as not all books

have been digitized. In addition, access to many of the academic journals can be gained only

through library subscriptions—they are not free online. Besides books, libraries are the location

for access to newspapers and magazines.[23]

Librarians are in the forefront of directing users to sources for research. As Sherman

notes, "their work involves guiding and educating visitors on how to find information, regardless

of whether it is in book or digital form." Moreover, because librarians have the expertise to find

information, they are able to help students find information in the most effective and efficient

manner.[24]

TAKING EFFECTIVE NOTES

As you gather your sources, you need to organize your research and take notes

effectively. One way to organize your research is by topic and subtopic. For example, if you are

writing a paper using the major theories as applied to a particular event in international relations,

you might want to have a folder labeled "theories" that contains all the articles and notes on the

books you have printed out. You also might want to have a folder that separates out the different

theories ("realism," "liberalism," and "constructivism"). If you are writing a paper on the

transition to democracy in Eastern Europe, you might want to have a folder on

"democratization," as well as separate folders for the countries in Eastern Europe that you might

be examining. Many journal articles are pdf files, such as those available through JSTOR, which

you can save on your computer. You can print them out and then make notes in the margin,

highlighting the main points of each article.

---

[23] Sherman, "33 Reasons Why Libraries and Librarians Are Still Extremely Important."
[24] Sherman, "33 Reasons Why Libraries and Librarians Are Still Extremely Important."

As for the actual act of taking notes, you need to figure out a system that works best for you and helps you keep track of the materials you have gathered. You might want to type notes into a computer file or write notes on note cards (using one card per author per article/book). Make sure to have the information for the complete citation (author's name, title of book or article, and so forth) (see Chapter 4 for details on proper citation). Be sure to put quotation marks around any direct quotes and indicate from which pages you got the information. You want to be sure that you are keeping track of direct quotes and paraphrases.

You might also consider the use of a citation (or "reference management") software package for your research. There are several such packages available for taking notes, formatting citations (including the major citation styles noted in Chapter 4), and building a bibliography. These software packages also allow the user to import citations from databases and websites, for example, JSTOR. Some of the most used software packages include EndNote, Mendeley, RefWorks, and Zotero. The box below provides a comparison of four citation software packages, found on the MIT Libraries website. Be sure to check your university's library to see if you can access and download the software.

"Overview of Citation Software at MIT: Managing Your References—Full Comparison of Citation Software"

	EndNote	**RefWorks**	**Zotero**	**Mendeley**
Type	Desktop client software; also has web interface, EndNote Web, through Web of	Web-based	Desktop software and browser add-on for Firefox, Chrome, and Safari	Desktop software and web-based. Works with IE, Firefox, Chrome

	Knowledge			and Safari
Learning curve	Takes longer to learn, but not difficult with training	Fairly quick to learn; many online user guides and demos	Quick to learn; simple design, many online user guides and demos	Quick to learn. pretty simple interface
Strengths?	Excellent for organizing citations for papers and theses Best option for major research projects, because it offers the most options for customization and formatting Most output styles for formatting Most customizable Can handle a large amount of references	Allows users to share citations Good for organizing citations for papers Web-based	Simple download of records Good for managing a variety of formats, including webpages Offers most functionality in a free, open-source product Downloads records from with several databases that don't work with EndNote and RefWorks, including Factiva, USPTO, Espacenet, & FreePatentsOnline.	Great for managing PDFs Has a social aspect. Can see what other users are reading and citing, find other members with common research interests. Does an excellent job of pulling citation metadata from pdfs Can share citations and documents with others
How does it work?	You export references from compatible databases into EndNote	You export references from compatible databases into RefWorks	Zotero can tell when you are looking at an item and shows an icon for it in the browser's URL bar. Click the icon to add the item to your Zotero references	You export references from compatible databases. Mendeley will also retrieve metadata for pdfs that are brought in
Does it have many output styles and bibliographic formats?	Yes, many popular styles and formats	Yes, many popular styles and formats	Yes, many popular styles and formats	Yes, many popular styles and formats
How simple is it to import	Simple to import records from most	Simple to import records	Very simple, as long as the resource is	Very simple using the

records?	research databases	from most research databases	compatible with Zotero, but you will want to verify that the records are complete after import	Mendeley browser plugin. However, the import doesn't work with as many databases as other products.
What kinds of records can you import and organize (pdfs, images, etc.)?	Can organize records for articles and books; pdfs and other file types can also be stored in the records. Can download pdfs in batches. pdfs aren't searchable.	Records for articles and books	Books, articles, patents, and webpages; can also store pdfs, web screenshots, files, and images in records. You can make pdfs searchable by choosing to index them in the preferences menu.	You can import bibliographic citations and pdfs. Can also manually add citations
Are records in your library viewable by others?	No.	Yes; users can share references in library with other RefWorks users	Yes. users can set up individual and group profiles and share records	Yes. users can set up groups to share references. Users can decide whether or not to make their library viewable by others
Can you export records to other citation software?	Yes	Yes	Yes	Yes. Export to EndNote XML, RIS and BibTeX
Is managing and maintaining a big library (1000 records) complicated?	Not complex; EndNote is best option for maintaining large libraries	Not complex, but it can be cumbersome to manage large libraries	No known problems. Need to purchase extra space for large collections.	No known problems. Need to purchase extra space for large collections.
Does it work with word processing software?	Clean integration with Word and powerful formatting and customization features; also works with Open Office and LaTex through BibTex	Works with Word through "Write-N-Cite" feature and LaTex through BibTex	Works with Word and Open Office; also works with LaTex through BibTex. You can create a list of Works Cited for Google Docs	Works with Word and OpenOffice.

Does it back up your records?	No	Yes	Yes, if you choose to back up or sync your Zotero library. A small amount of storage is free.	Yes
Other important features	pdf file management and organization features	Since it's web-based, you're not limited to a single machine	If you back up records, you can sync multiple computers Integrated with work on web that you do Fastest download of records Saves snapshot of web pages Allows users to highlight text and take notes on page Allows users to tag records	Very good for collaborative work Has a good pdf reader that enables highlighting and comments

Source: "Overview of Citation Software at MIT: Managing Your References," MIT Libraries, http://libguides.mit.edu/content.php?pid=55486&sid=427307.

___

When you have gathered this research, you should look over your notes and begin to think about the connections between the various pieces of scholarship. How are they similar? What themes emerge? What is left out? How does the research help you test your independent and dependent variables? Are you able to answer your research question?

CONCLUSION

You need to know when to stop researching and reading. This is an art form. There is always one more book, journal article, or newspaper article to read, but you can never read it all. It is easy to get immersed in lots of research, but at some point you will need to stop the research process and get started on writing the paper (especially in light of the fact that your professor has given you a deadline!). One way to know that you have read enough on your topic is that you consistently see the references for repeated works by other scholars. In other words, if the same author is cited in many of the other sources you have found, you can rest assured that you have done due diligence in familiarizing yourself with that literature and have found credible sources.

In concluding this chapter, think about the ways in which you are contributing to new knowledge as you research your topic and begin to write.

Chapter 3

Writing, Rewriting, Revising, and Editing

Now that you have completed the bulk of the research, it is time to start writing. Most researchers spend a lot of time researching before they begin to write. Crucially, it is also a matter of knowing when to stop researching and begin writing. For students this is particularly important because of term deadlines—if you have a paper due at the end of the term, you will need to make sure that you have organized your time effectively. This is where your time management skills come into play. It is easy to get engrossed in the research and postpone the writing process. However, you do not want to have spent the bulk of the term doing all the research and then find yourself starting to write the paper a day or two before the paper is due to your professor. Moreover, procrastinating on writing a paper will lead to a poorly written paper. Professors can tell when a paper has been thrown together, when a student has not taken the time or effort to produce a good piece of writing. Good writing means lots of it—drafts, drafts, and more drafts—before having the finished product ready to be submitted. This chapter covers the writing process: from writing an outline; to writing, revising, editing, and proofreading; to formatting the paper as preparation for submission to your professor.

WRITING: DRAFTS, DRAFTS, AND MORE DRAFTS

The key to organizing all the research into a good paper is to make an outline before you begin any serious writing. <u>Again: an outline is key!</u> An outline helps you organize the parts of the paper and also determine where all the research you have gathered fits. The structure of a typical research paper discussed in Chapter 1 is a good start for an outline, but you need to add the parts to it now that you have done the research. Using an example paper topic, the causes of World War I,[1] the outline might look something like this:

    I.   Introduction: The causes of World War I

          A. Research question: What Caused World War I?

          B. Thesis Statement: The rise of Germany led to the outbreak of World War I

          C. Road Map of paper

    II.   Literature Review

          A. Introductory paragraph on the major theories/explanations of the causes of World War I

          B. Main variables/factors that scholars have argued to explain the causes of the war

          C. Restate your thesis statement

    III.   Research Design/Methodology/Hypothesis

          A. Hypothesis: The rise of Germany led to the outbreak of World War I

          B. Case study approach

    IV.   Factors to be Considered as Applied to the Case Study

          A. Rise of Germany

              i. Threat to the European balance of power

              ii. Germany's naval program

          B. Economic Change and Competition in Europe

          C. Alliance System

---

[1] See Spiegel et al, *World Politics in a New Era*, 5th ed. (New York: Oxford University Press, 2012), 82–88, for a discussion of the causes of World War I using the levels-of-analysis framework in international relations.

                    i. Shift from multipolar to increasingly rigid bipolar system

                  ii. Formation of the Triple Alliance and Triple Entente

        D. Nationalism

        E. Imperialism

        F. Cult of the Offensive

                  i. Influence of offensive military doctrines

V.   Analysis of the Evidence: your findings

VI.   Conclusion

        A. Restate the research question

        B. Restate the evidence and your findings

        C. Tell whether the evidence supported your thesis

Now that you have a working outline, you can gather your research notes and begin to write the parts of the paper. But you may find that there are holes in your research that need to be filled based on your outline. That is okay—the working outline gets you started and provides direction for conducting additional research if needed and writing the paper.

Writing the Paper

In writing a research paper (or any written assignment), there are basic rules of grammar and spelling that should be followed. There are reasons for such rules, or conventions, as they allow for clear and effective communication. What happens when commas and apostrophes ("it's" versus "its") are used incorrectly? How does doing so change the meaning of a sentence? This does not mean that the rules do not change; sometimes they do. For example, splitting of infinitives once was considered a violation of a convention, and so one would write "to go boldly." However, the convention of not splitting infinitives is no longer strictly adhered to anymore, and you will find, as the *Star Trek* television show's opening statement claims: ". . . *to boldly go* where no man has gone before."

For the most part, however, there are conventions and rules for grammar and spelling that are important to know as you write. That said, there are many good style guides available in which you should invest to help you become a better writer. One of the classics is *The Elements of Style* by William Strunk Jr. and E. B. White (see Chapter 5 for other suggested works). Also, invest in a dictionary and a thesaurus. You will find them helpful resources as you write—they will enhance your vocabulary and help in finding the appropriate words to express your thoughts and ideas.

Here is a brief list of several conventions that matter in writing:

1. <u>Avoid colloquialisms, clichés, slang, and any casual language</u>. This is a research paper, and you want to demonstrate formality and professionalism. Using colloquialisms, clichés, slang, and all-around casual language lessens the impact and import of your argument and overall paper.

2. <u>Use gender-neutral language</u>. Gender is a social construction of what is considered feminine and what is considered masculine and the expected roles that men and women play. Because men/masculinity is valued in most societies more highly than women/femininity, there is an inherent bias in using "he" to refer to both men and women. This has been the standard convention, but the use of "he" privileges both men and males. It is better to use the plural, "their," or use the word "people" in place of "he/him" and "she/her."

Rather than writing: "Whereas it is essential, if *man* is not to be compelled to have recourse, as a last resort, to rebellion against tyranny and oppression, that human rights should be protected by the rule of law…" (emphasis added),[2] write: "if *people* are not to be compelled. . . ."

Additionally, sometimes inanimate objects are referred to in gendered terms, as in this example: "The United States is the world's largest economy. *She* also has the world's most technologically advanced military." Avoid using "he/him" and "she/her" when referring to inanimate objects. States, for example, are not male or female.

3. <u>Use of quotation marks</u>. In using quotation marks (" "), the rule of thumb is to use them when the quote is not longer than four lines (also known as a *run-in quotation*). When there are five lines or more, use a *block quotation*.[3] A block quotation is indented, and no quotation marks are used (sometimes it is single-spaced). Here is a comparison between a run-in quotation and a block quotation.

Run-in quotation:

According to Spiegel et al., "Some argue that globalization has begun to marginalize nation-states."[4]

Block quotation:

According to Spiegel et al.,

> Some argue that globalization has begun to marginalize nation-states. As international regimes, regional and subregional trading blocs, NGOs [nongovernmental organizations], and MNCs [multinational corporations] promote and take advantage of relaxed constraints on the movement of goods, capital, and labor, states necessarily cede some of

---

[2] United Nations, "United Nations Declaration of Human Rights," http://www.un.org/en/documents/udhr/index.shtml.
[3] Kate L. Turabian, *Student's Guide to Writing College Papers*, 4th ed., revised by Gregory G. Colomb, Joseph M. Williams, and the University of Chicago Press Editorial Staff (Chicago: University of Chicago Press, 2010), 93.
[4] Spiegel, et al., *World Politics in a New Era*, 7.

their authority to these other groups. Fragmentation, on the other hand, is driven precisely by local, domestic, and regional social, environmental, political, and economic considerations, thus impeding globalization by forcing government attention back home to constituents, interest groups, and local imperatives.[5]

If there is a quote within a quote, a single quotation mark is used for the internal quoted word or phrase. For example:

Spiegel et al. note, "Almost six decades after the end of China's civil war, the People's Republic of China claims that the self-governing island of Taiwan is part of China and refers to it as a 'renegade province.'"[6]

In the Spiegel et al. book, "renegade province" has the double quotation marks, but because a sentence is being quoted from that book here, the double quotation marks go around the whole sentence (as it is a direct quote), and the single quotation marks go around the word/phrase, "renegade province," that had the double quotes in the original. Also remember that the quotation marks bracket the punctuation: "renegade province." Here, the quotation mark goes after the period (.").

4. <u>Tense agreement</u>. If you are writing about something historical, it is in the past, and therefore the past tense should be used. Also, be sure that your tenses are in agreement: do not use both the past and the present. For example, write: "Napoleon *sought* to expand the French empire and *did* so by invading Spain." Do not write: "Napoleon *seeks* to expand the French Empire and *did* so by invading Spain."

---

[5] Spiegel, et al., *World Politics in a New Era*, 7.
[6] Spiegel, et al., *World Politics in a New Era*, 220.

5. <u>Citations</u>. Citations come in three forms: in-text (also known as parenthetical citations), footnotes (found at the bottom of the page), and endnotes (found at the end of the paper and before the bibliography/reference page). Parenthetical notes are "in-text," usually employing the author-date system (Jones 2012). They are not numbered. Footnotes and endnotes are numbered consecutively (1, 2, 3, . . .) through to the end of the paper. The numbering does not restart on each new page. For example, if page 1 has three citations—1, 2, and 3—the next citation should be number 4 even if it is on page 2 of your paper. Further, more than one source can be included in a single citation. The formatting of the citations differs from that of the entries in the bibliography/reference page (see Chapter 4 for the proper format for the different types of citation styles). At least one citation should be included in each paragraph of your paper (except the introduction and conclusion or parts of the paper in which it is your own analysis).

The Introduction

Writing the *introduction* can sometimes be the hardest part of the paper but often the most useful even if it is a draft. Writing the introduction can help frame the paper, forcing the writer to be clear and concise. Having a working introduction is fine—it can always (and most likely should) be revised. Once you have finished writing the paper, however, you should go back to the introduction and reread it to yourself, especially the first sentence and paragraph that introduces the reader to the rest of the paper. As Jennifer L. Hochschild astutely notes, "Every book, article, or journal issue has only one first sentence and paragraph. So it is essential to get them right (which often implies that the first sentence is written many times, most crucially after the rest of the document is finished)."[7] This holds true for a college research paper too.

_____

[7] Jennifer L. Hochschild, "Writing Introductions," in *Publishing Political Science: APSA Guide to Writing and Publishing*, ed. Stephen Yoder (Washington, DC: American Political Science Association, 2008), 93.

Here is an example of the introductory paragraph to a journal article:

"The Soviet Union's collapse transformed the international system dramatically, but there has been no corresponding change in U.S. grand strategy. In terms of ambitions, interests, and alliances, the United States is following the same grand strategy it pursued from 1945 until 1991: that of preponderance. Whether this strategy will serve U.S. interests in the early twenty-first century is problematic. Hence, in this article my purpose is to stimulate a more searching debate about future U.S. grand strategic options. To accomplish this, I compare the strategy of preponderance to a proposed alternative grand strategy: offshore balancing."[8]

The author has written a paragraph with a clear topic sentence—that with the end of the Cold War, U.S. grand strategy has not changed. The author then asserts that this is a challenging strategy for America's future and introduces the reader to the main point of the article: to compare two strategies available to the United States—preponderance and offshore balancing.

The Literature Review

When writing the *literature review*, as noted in Chapter 1, keep in mind that you are categorizing the scholarship (literature) on your particular topic. As Knopf and McMenamin state, it "is not a succession of book reviews. It should not simply summarize, item by item, each publication you have read. A literature review should *not* have the following structure: paragraph 1 notes that book A says X; paragraph 2 notes that article B says Y; paragraph 3 notes that book

---

[8] Christopher Layne, "From Preponderance to Offshore Balancing: America's Future Grand Strategy," *International Security* 22, 1 (Summer 1997), 86. Copyright © 1997, Massachusetts Institute of Technology.

C says Z; etc." (emphasis in original).[9] A literature review is a means to situate your research within the larger scholarship. In doing so, you will want to organize the literature by approaches or theories (rather than by authors or publications). In the case of international relations, for example, this could mean organizing by theories (e.g., realism, liberalism, constructivism). The literature review would then discuss realism (and its variants, such as classical realism and structural realism), liberalism (and its variants: classical liberalism and liberal institutionalism), and constructivism (such as critical theory, post-postmodernism, and feminist theory). In discussing the literature, you will need to discuss the theories' claims and their limitations and then show how your research connects, or fits, with one or some or all of the theories. In essence, the literature review is meant to demonstrate your understanding of the existing scholarship.

As you continue to write the other parts of the paper, keep in mind that this is a draft. It is better to get your ideas written down and then rework the paper later (that is where the revising step comes in, although some writers revise and edit as they write). Also realize that it is always easier to cut what you have written, so put pen to paper, or fingers to keyboard, and get writing!

If you are using a computer to write, you may want to save your versions in different files so that you have a record of the various drafts (one suggestion is to give each file a name and date: "draft 23 March 2013," "draft 5 April 2013," "final version 30 April 2013," and so on). Be sure, though, that as you write, you are inserting your sources/citations (and hence the advice to have good note-taking skills, with all the bibliographic information with your notes, as advised in Chapter 2). You do not want to find yourself in the difficult situation of tracking down your sources when you get to the final version of the paper.

Some other things to consider as you write (and rewrite, revise, and edit too):

---

[9] Jeffrey W. Knopf and Iain McMenamin, "How to Write a Literature Review," in *Publishing Political Science: APSA Guide to Writing and Publishing*, ed. Stephen Yoder (Washington, DC: American Political Science Association, 2008), 111.

- Write clear and crisp sentences (and make sure they are complete sentences, not fragments).

- Keep your sentences short. If you have a particularly long sentence that runs several lines, break it up into several sentences.

- Use the active, not passive, voice (e.g., "The United States invaded Iraq," not "Iraq was invaded by the United States.").

- Avoid using long, complicated words.

- Have a topic sentence that sets the tone for each paragraph.

- Make sure to transition between paragraphs so that the paragraphs flow together.

- Use headings and subheadings (which describe what the section is about) to separate sections in the paper and allow for smoother transitions.

REVISING

Now that you have completed a draft (or drafts) of your paper, you need to do the next step: revise (of course, some writers prefer to revise as they write). It is at this point that you want to make sure that you have written an effective and persuasive research paper, convincing the reader of your argument. One recommendation is to put the paper away for a few days before starting the revising process. This way, you can come back to it with a set of fresh eyes. You can see the paper as a whole, as well as its parts. It is also recommended that you revise a hard copy of the paper rather than work on the computer screen. You can write editorial comments and notes in the margins of the hard copy (perhaps use a pen with a bold, contrast color such as red or green rather than black or blue ink). Seeing the paper literally on paper helps you see it as a whole rather than scrolling down on the screen. Of course, you may want to do your revisions on the computer, using track changes and the comments commands as you revise your paper.

When you are ready to revise, some strategies include reading the paper slowly to yourself so that you can really see your own words and the rhythm of your sentences and paragraphs. You also might want to read the paper out loud to yourself—then you really do <u>hear</u> what you have written. As Thomas Kane asserts: "Ears are often more trustworthy than eyes. They detect an awkwardness in sentence structure or a jarring repetition the eyes pass over. Even if you're not exactly sure what's wrong, you *hear* that something is, and you can tinker with the sentences until they sound better" (emphasis in original).[10]

As you revise, ask yourself these questions:

- Does this sentence sound right?

- Does this particular word fit in this sentence?

- Are the transitions from one paragraph to the next clear?

- Does each paragraph convey what I want it to?

- Is the introduction clear?

- Is the conclusion clear?

It is also at this time that you can and should be brutal about cutting or deleting parts of the paper that are extraneous. It is easy to feel that you have done all this research and have written pages and pages of text and thus cannot bear to take any of it out. You must be willing to be ruthless—cut whatever is unnecessary, redundant, and irrelevant. Do not consider what you have written to be so valuable and important that it must remain in the final version of your paper just because you spent time writing *that* paragraph or *that* sentence. Rather, part of the research

---

[10] Thomas S. Kane, *The Oxford Essential Guide to Writing* (New York: Berkley Books, 2000), 37.

and writing process is to know when to keep material and when to delete it. Remember: clear, concise, and effective writing demonstrates your written communication and analytical skills to the reader.

EDITING THE PAPER

Editing is not the same as rewriting and revising a paper. Once the paper has been written and revised (and revised yet again), you are now at the final draft stage. You will need to edit the paper to make sure that it is polished, free of grammatical and spelling errors, for example. Both the content and the presentation of a paper matter. It is important to be aware that it is not just *what you write* (the substantive content) but also *how you write it* (presentation). A good paper is one that reads well, is organized, and is written clearly and coherently, with transition sentences from one paragraph to the next. Think of your reader: Does she or he have to struggle to figure out what your paper is trying to say and where it is going? Does the paper read well and make sense? You want to make sure that all your words are spelled correctly. Word processing programs have spell check and grammar check functions, and so such errors should be eliminated at all costs. At the same time, however, do not rely solely on the word processor's spell check function to catch everything—you need to make sure that you have spelled the words correctly. For example, here is a sentence in which the words are spelled correctly but one of the words is not spelled correctly in the context of the sentence:

> *There are for major theories in international relations that are used to explain the causes of interstate wars.*

Here the word "for" is spelled correctly (in other words, there is a word "for" and this is one way it is spelled), but in the context of this sentence it is not spelled correctly (it should read "four").

The spell check function would not (and did not) catch this error. Style guides are available that list commonly misspelled and misused words. An example of a commonly misused word is "less." According to Strunk and White, "**Less**. Should not be misused for *fewer*. . . . *Less* refers to quantity, *fewer* to number. 'His troubles are less than mine' means 'His troubles are not so great as mine.' 'His troubles are fewer than mine' means 'His troubles are not so numerous as mine'" (emphasis in original).[11] It is recommended that you buy a style guide if spelling and word usage are not your strong suit!

As with the writing and revising process, you must be willing to remove extraneous text, whether whole paragraphs or individual sentences. You need to check for clarity and organization. Are there paragraphs that need to be rearranged? Are there citations missing? You want to have a paper that reads well and shows the work and effort you have put into the assignment.

THE NITTY-GRITTY: FORMATTING THE PAPER IN PREPARATION FOR SUBMISSION

Formatting the paper is also a very important part of the writing process. It is part of the presentation aspect of a paper that professors consider when reading—and, importantly, grading—a paper. Professors will give instructions on the formatting requirements, and most usually have the same requirements (they all want set margins, page length, pagination, spacing, citations, and a bibliography). The formatting features are found on word processing systems, and you should familiarize yourself with them.

1. **Margins**: Usually the margins are 1" on all four sides, with the left margin justified.

---

[11] William Strunk Jr. and E. B. White, *The Elements of Style*, 4th ed. (New York: Longman Publishing, 2000), 51.

2. **Spacing**: Double-space the text; single-space the footnotes/endnotes and any indented/block quotations.

3. **Font**: 12 point (usually Times Roman or Courier) for the text; 10 point for the footnotes. If your paper length is shorter than that required for the assignment, increasing the font size is not going to fool the professor. The standard font size for most articles and books submitted to a publisher is 12 point—and so professors are well aware of what other font sizes look like. The footnotes are usually a slightly smaller font size (10 point) and are usually single spaced.

4. **Pagination**: Papers have page numbers. If the staple comes apart, you do not want your professor trying to figure out the order of your pages in putting the paper back together again. Page numbers are written consecutively starting on the first page (1, 2, 3, . . .).

5. **Headings and Subheadings**: Transitioning between sections of a paper can be difficult. The use of subheadings and headings, which describe what the section is about, is a good way to help with those transitions. There are different levels of headings: primary, secondary, and tertiary. The different levels are indicated in different kinds of type. The key is to be consistent. A primary heading might be in bold and all uppercase; a secondary heading might be in bold and lowercase and uppercase; and a tertiary heading might be italicized and in lowercase and uppercase. Here is an example:

    THEORIES IN INTERNATIONAL RELATIONS

    Realism

    Classical Realism

    Structural (or Neo-) Realism

    Liberalism

Classical Liberalism

Liberal Institutionalism

6. **Indent Paragraphs:** Paragraphs should be indented five spaces. Use the "tab" key on your word processor, which will automatically indent.

7. **Bibliography (or References or Works Cited) page**: All sources used in the paper must be noted on the bibliography page. It is found after the text of the paper and the endnotes (if a paper is using endnotes rather than footnotes or parenthetical citations), basically the last section of a paper. The bibliography is alphabetized by author's last name and includes all information: name of book or article, journal title, volume and issue number, date of publication, location of publication, and entire page range for a journal article. Do not number or use bullet points on a bibliography. Examples of the different styles are provided in Chapter 4.

8. **Title Page**: Some professors also may require a title page. The title page should have the title of your paper, your name, the instructor's name, and the course title, as well as the due date of the assignment. All of this should be centered on the page. A sample title page looks like the one that follows:

The Causes of World War I

by

Jane Doe

Political Science 100

Professor Susan Jones

December 10, 2013

If no title page is required, you should make sure that your name is always at the top of each page of your paper, in the corner. Word processing programs have the Header function (a header is at the top of a page, and a footer is located at the bottom—where the page number sometimes goes) that you can use for inserting your name throughout the paper.

PROOFREADING

You are almost done. You have researched your puzzle, and you have written the paper and revised and edited it. There is one more step: proofreading. This occurs on the last draft, now that the editing has been done. When proofreading, you are checking for any last possible errors in sentence structure. You want to make sure there are no spelling or punctuation errors. You want to make sure that the pages are paginated and that the margins are set. Be sure that there are no headings left at the bottom of a page without any text beneath them (see the "widow and orphan" function on your word processor; this makes sure there is no heading left by itself without text immediately underneath and that no single word is left on a page at the top).

To submit a paper that has not been proofread for errors is sloppy and lazy. The reader will be distracted and not focused on the argument and evidence you are providing. You are trying to make a case for your thesis to convince the reader that your argument is well supported. As Scott and Garrison astutely observe: "Above all else, remember that your paper represents you."[12] This is your last opportunity to make sure that your paper is presentable. You have worked hard on this project, and you want to make sure that it properly represents that hard work.

---

[12] Gregory M. Scott and Stephen M. Garrison, *The Political Science Student Writer's Manual*, 7th ed. (New York: Longman, 2012), 29.

GETTING FEEDBACK FROM OTHERS

Another helpful suggestion comes in the form of feedback from others, in this case your

peers as well as a writing center (or its equivalent) at your college or university. Having a friend

read your paper (regardless of which stage: writing, revising, editing, or proofreading) is a great

way to have an objective eye read your work and comment on it. If what you have written does

not make sense to your friends, the paper most likely will not make sense to your professor

either.

Most colleges and universities have writing centers specifically designed to help students

work through the writing process, whether a research paper, honors thesis, or résumé. At a

writing center, tutors or counselors are trained to help students in all stages of the writing

process. Some writing centers may offer walk-in appointments as well as regular meetings.

Regardless, you should check out your school's writing center about the services it has to offer.

Getting assistance early is important. Showing up for a consultation a day or two before your

paper is due will not serve you well. Take advantage of the writing services that your college or

university has available to help you.

CONCLUSION

The writing process is one that can bring feelings of being overwhelmed and stressed.

But as this book has shown thus far, it need not be so. In fact, the research and writing process

can bring a sense of joy and accomplishment. Finding a research question, testing a hypothesis,

conducting the research, and writing about one's findings to share with others and contribute to

new knowledge are important skills, including written communication skills and critical thinking skills. The art of writing, rewriting and revising, and editing matters for communicating

effectively and clearly to the reader. The last step in the process is ensuring that the citations and

references are in order and in the proper format. That is the focus of the next chapter.

Chapter 4

Citations and Bibliography

Knowledge is not produced in a vacuum. As was noted in Chapter 1, the production of knowledge is an ongoing endeavor. Scholars write and publish their works, and then others read and evaluate those works, adding their own contributions to the scholarly literature. In building on the work of others, those works have to be acknowledged. That means there needs to be citations. Citations matter so that others can go to your sources for their research, just as you sought out the research of others as you engaged in the research process in the attempt to answer your research question. Readers can then see the path of your research and evaluate the credibility and legitimacy of those sources.

The body of knowledge of others must be cited, whether in a direct quote (word for word, verbatim), paraphrasing (putting the author's ideas in your own words), or borrowing the ideas of others. Failure to attribute a quote, a paraphrase, or the borrowing of an idea from someone else is considered plagiarism. It is a serious offense in the academic world to take the ideas or words of another without proper attribution, and it is considered a violation of academic integrity.

Some information is considered "fair use" or "common knowledge," for example, "the sun always rises in the east and sets in the west," "the Earth is round," "World War I began in 1914 and ended in 1918." In these instances, citations are not needed. However, if in doubt, cite—it is always better to err on the side of citing. Do not hesitate to ask your professor about citing.

To make sure that you have the correct citation and source information, be sure to insert your citations in your paper as you take notes. You should also insert your citations as you write, regardless of whether it is the first, second, fifth, or final draft. The question then arises: How to cite? This chapter addresses the topic of how to cite, specifically the three common citation styles used in political science. The chapter also provides examples of the three styles using the kinds of research that political scientists employ in their research (i.e., books, articles, magazines, newspapers, online sources). Examples of the corresponding bibliographic entry are also included.

CITING DIRECT QUOTES, PARAPHRASE, AND IDEAS

As was noted above, you need to cite whenever you quote directly from a source, paraphrase a source, or borrow the ideas of a source. Here are three examples:

Direct quote: "Students today live in an era of fragmentation in which the interests of individual nation-states have been challenged by the competing ideals of globalization" (Spiegel et al., 2012, xxiii).

Paraphrase: According to Spiegel et al., in the contemporary period states are faced with challenges from both fragmentation and globalization (Spiegel et al., 2012, xxiii).

Borrowing idea: Spiegel et al. (2012) demonstrate that fragmentation and globalization are affecting states in a range of issue areas, including security (weapons of mass destruction, terrorism), economics (trade relations), and social (health, population, migration) issues.

CITATION STYLES

Three main forms of citation styles are used: APA, MLA, and Chicago. These three forms are also, in some ways, discipline-specific. The MLA (Modern Language Association) style is the main style used in the humanities. The APA (American Psychological Association) style is used in the quantitative social sciences. The Chicago (University of Chicago Press) style is used in the humanities and the qualitative social sciences.[1] These three correspond to the different styles you probably have seen in your research: parenthetical (in-text), footnotes, and endnotes. In addition to the citations found in the text of your paper itself, you need to include your sources in a bibliography or references list (sometimes called a "works-cited" list).

Because political scientists use research from books, academic journal articles, magazines, newspapers, Internet sources, and so forth, this section provides examples of each of these in the three different citation styles and their corresponding bibliographic/references/works-cited page entries. As you go through the various examples provided in this section, keep in mind the location of the publication date, whether an author's first name is spelled out (is only the initial of the first name written?), and which kinds of punctuation are being used to separate the information (period? comma? colon?). The three styles do differ. Importantly, though, for all three styles, in the bibliography/references page/works-cited list include three main pieces of information: author, title, and publication information.[2]

---

[1] For the different styles, see Lucille Charlton and Mark Charlton, *Thomson Guide to Research and Writing in Political Science* (Toronto: Thomson Nelson, 2006), 39; Joseph Gibaldi, *MLA Handbook for Writers of Research Papers*, 5th ed. (New York: The Modern Language Association of America, 1999), 115; *MLA Handbook for Writers of Research Papers*, 7th ed. (New York: The Modern Language Association of America, 2009); Kate L. Turabian, *Student's Guide to Writing College Papers*, 4th ed., revised by Gregory G. Colomb, Joseph M. Williams, and the University of Chicago Press Editorial Staff (Chicago: University of Chicago Press, 2010), 147; *The Chicago Manual of Style: The Essential Guide for Writers, Editors, and Publishers*, 16th ed. (Chicago: University of Chicago Press, 2010), chapters 14 and 15.

[2] Turabian, *Student's Guide to Writing College Papers*, 173.

Although all three citation styles are acceptable (meaning they are commonly used in academic scholarship), always consult your professor for the citation style that is required or that the professor prefers that you use. Moreover, it is not expected that you have all these various rules memorized, so do consult a style guide for reference as you write.

APA Style and References List[3]

The APA style uses parenthetical citations. These are in the text and are bracketed in parentheses (hence "parenthetical" citations). The author's last name, the year of publication (this is the copyright date), and the page number(s), in that order, are placed within the parentheses. A comma is used after the author's name as well as after the date. The references list, which is alphabetized, provides the rest of the reference information (title of work, location of publisher, name of publisher, date of publication, and page numbers, if applicable). If the reference entry is longer than one line, indent the second line. The reference list is single-spaced for each entry, with a double space between entries.[4]

Here is an example of the citation within the text (parenthetical) using the APA style, with the author, date, page number (using "p." or "pp." if there is more than one page):

"To begin with, nineteenth-century Europe helped to standardize the practice of fully *excluding* women from political authority around the world" (Towns, 2010, p. 187).

---

[3] This section drawn from Turabian, *Student's Guide to Writing College Papers*, chapter 20. For more on the APA style, see that chapter. See also: Purdue Online Writing Lab, "Reference List: Basic Rules: APA Style," Purdue University, http://owl.english.purdue.edu/owl/resource/560/05/.
[4] Turabian, *Student's Guide to Writing College Papers*, 198-99.

Or, if you are naming the author in the text, you place the date of publication after the author's

name. The page number follows the quote and is placed in parentheses, followed by the

punctuation (in this case, a period):[5]

As Towns (2010) argues, "To begin with, nineteenth-century Europe helped to

standardize the practice of fully *excluding* women from political authority around the

world" (p. 187).

Book with one author

(Towns, 2010, p. 187).

For the references list, the author's last name goes first (inverted: last name, initial of first and

middle names), followed by the publication date (in parentheses), title of publication, which is

italicized (and note that only the first word of the title is capitalized; all other words are

lowercase), location of the publisher (city—and state if the city is not a familiar one), and name

of the publisher. Note that a period is used after each piece of information.[6]

Towns, A. E. (2010). *Women and states: Norms and hierarchies in international society*. New

York: Cambridge University Press.

Book with two or three authors

(Ackerly & True, 2010, p. 15)

---

[5] Turabian, *Student's Guide to Writing College Papers*, 200.
[6] Purdue Online Writing Lab, "Reference List: Basic Rules: APA Style"; Turabian, *Student's Guide to Writing College Papers*, 203.

For the references list, all the authors' last names are listed first, followed by the initials of the first, and if applicable, middle names (i.e., inverted: last name, initial of first and middle names). Use an ampersand (&) between the two authors' names. If there are three authors, the ampersand goes only between the second and third authors. The date of publication follows (in parentheses), then the title of publication (in italics), location of publisher, and name of publisher.[7]

Ackerly, B., & True, J. (2010). *Doing feminist research in political and social science*. New

   York: Palgrave Macmillan.

Book with four or more authors

(Spiegel, Matthews, Taw, & Williams, 2012, p. 45)

For subsequent citations in the text, one can use "et al." (Latin for "and others")

(Spiegel et al., 2012, p. 45)

As this book is also a fifth edition, you will need to provide that information as well. It is placed after the title of the book, in parentheses. "Edition" is abbreviated to "ed."

Spiegel, S. L., Matthews, E. G., Taw, J. M., & Williams, K. P. (2012). *World politics in a new*

   era (5th ed.). New York: Oxford University Press.

---

[7] Turabian, *Student's Guide to Writing College Papers*, 203.

An edited book

(Berger & Huntington, 2002)

As this is an edited book and the citation is for the entire book, the abbreviation (Ed. for a single

editor, or Eds. for more than one editor) is placed after the names of the editors, and before the

date of publication.[8]

Berger, P. L., & Huntington, S. P. (Eds.). 2002. *Many globalizations: Cultural diversity in the*

   contemporary world. New York: Oxford University Press.

Chapter in an edited book

If you are citing a specific chapter and author in an edited book, you need to provide the

information for that author and chapter both in the citation and in the references list. When it

comes to citing chapters in a book, the important thing to keep in mind is that you are citing the

author of the chapter, not the editor. Thus, in the example below, as Berger is the author of the

chapter being cited, his name is written, not the editors, Berger & Huntington.

(Berger, 2002, p. 14)

In the references list, the title of the chapter is neither italicized nor has quotation marks around

it. The word "In" is inserted after the chapter title but before the names of the editors. The

abbreviation for editor(s), (Ed.) or (Eds.), follows, then a comma, and then the title of the book.

The page numbers of the entire chapter are placed in parentheses, followed by the publication

---

[8] Turabian, *Student's Guide to Writing College Papers*, 209.

location and publisher name. Again, note that Berger, the author of Chapter 1 of the edited book, is being cited.

Berger, P. L. (2002). The cultural dynamics of globalization. In P. L. Berger & S. P.

Huntington (Eds.), *Many globalizations: Cultural diversity in the contemporary world*

(pp 1–16). Oxford: Oxford University Press.

Journal article

(Ikenberry, 2011, pp. 57–58)

There are no italics or quotation marks around the title of the journal article (and only the first word of the article title is capitalized, including the first word of the subtitle; all other words are lower case).[9] The journal title is italicized (and important words are capitalized), followed by a comma, volume number, issue number (in parentheses), comma, and complete page range of the article.

Ikenberry, G. J. (2011). The future of the liberal world order: Internationalism after

America. *Foreign Affairs*, 90 (3), 56–68.

Magazine article

(Di Giovanni, 2011, p. 47)

---

[9] Purdue Online Writing Lab, "Reference List: Basic Rules: APA Style."

The date follows the author's name and the year comes first, followed by a comma and then the month and day. The title of the article does not have quotation marks around it, while the title of the magazine is italicized. List all the page numbers of a magazine article even if they are not consecutively ordered[10] (perhaps there is an advertisement on one of the pages, and so the pages for the article are not consecutive).

Di Giovanni, J. (2011, June 6). The making of a monster. *TIME*, 46–49.

Newspaper article

(Gorman, 2011, p. A4)

Note that the year of publication precedes the month and day in the reference entry, with a comma used after the year and before the month and day. There are no quotation marks around the headline; the name of the newspaper is italicized.[11]

Gorman, S. (2011, June 6). Cyberspies target China experts. *The Wall Street Journal*, p. A4.

Internet source

(USAID, 2013)

In the references list you include the author, date of publication (give year first; date is placed in parentheses followed by a period), title, and source (this can be the URL or the digital-object-

---

[10] Turabian, *Student's Guide to Writing College Papers*, 207.
[11] Turabian, *Student's Guide to Writing College Papers*, 207.

identifier, or DOI). If using the URL, write "Retrieved from" followed by the URL address. If using the DOI, just write: "doi:" followed by the address (note there is a colon after "doi"). The DOI "is a unique string of letters, numbers, and symbols assigned to a published work to identify content and provide a consistent link to its location on the Internet." A period is not placed after the URL or DOI.[12]

U.S. Agency for International Development. (2013, May 17). Conflict Mitigation and
     Prevention. Retrieved from http://www.usaid.gov/what-we-do/working-crises-and-
     conflict/conflict-mitigation-and-prevention

Other things to keep in mind as you cite and write using the APA style:

- Sometimes authors have the same last name, and so you will need to indicate in the in-text citation the different authors by using their first initials (J. Smith, 2011).

- If you are citing more than one work by the same author published in the same year, you will need to differentiate the publications by using a, b, c, and so on, after the date. To determine which work is designated a, b, c, and so on, you list the works alphabetically by title of the article or book.[13] For example, if you have cited Jane Smith, who published a book in 2011 and a journal article in the same year, you need to indicate one as (Smith, 2011a) and the other as (Smith, 2011b), based on the alphabetical title of the article and/or book. This a, b, c system will need to correspond with the references list; thus, when you refer to Smith, 2011a in the references list, Smith (2011a) will mean that citation.

---

[12] American Psychological Association, "Quick Answers-References: Websites," accessed June 3, 2013, http://www.apastyle.org/learn/quick-guide-on-references.aspx#Websites.
[13] Turabian, *Student's Guide to Writing College Papers*, 202.

- If you are citing more than one work by the same author in a citation, you will need to
  write the author's last name followed by the dates, in chronological order (starting with
  the oldest work listed first) of year of publication, separating each entry by a comma
  (Smith, 1991, 1992, 2005, 2010). When it comes to the references list, you will list the
  author's publications in chronological order, starting with the earliest work first.[14] After
  the first entry, all subsequent entries by the same author(s) will be set with a 3-em dash
  rather than repeating the author's name for each entry.

Spiegel, S. L., Matthews, E. G., Taw, J. M., & Williams, K. P. (2009). *World politics in a*
        new era (4th ed.). New York: Oxford University Press.

---. (2012). *World politics in a new era* (5th ed.). New York: Oxford University Press.

- If you are citing several authors in the same cite, you will need to write all the authors'
  last names and dates of publication. The authors are listed alphabetically.[15]

- If a publication is monthly, indicate the month (spell out the month, do not abbreviate). If
  the publication is weekly or daily, you need to include the day (2013, March 5).[16]

MLA Style and Works-Cited List[17]

The MLA style calls for the author-page in-text system and a works-cited list at the end

of the paper. In the citation, the author's last name and page number are placed within the

---

[14] Purdue Online Writing Lab, "Reference List: Basic Rules: APA Style."

[15] American Psychological Association, "How do you cite two or more references within the same parentheses?" accessed May 24, 2013, http://www.apastyle.org/learn/faqs/references-in-parentheses.aspx.

[16] Turabian, *Student's Guide to Writing College Papers*, 203.

[17] This section drawn from Gibaldi, *MLA Handbook for Writers of Research Papers*, chapters 4 and 5; *MLA Handbook for Writers of Research Papers*, 7th ed., chapters 5 and 6; Turabian, *Student's Guide to Writing College Papers*, chapter 19. For more on the MLA style, see these works.

parentheses. The date is omitted in the citation, and there is no comma after the author's name. In the works-cited page, all major words are capitalized, even those in the subtitle; book titles are italicized. In addition, the MLA now requires entries to indicate the type of publication medium (e.g., print, web). So, do keep an eye out for the differences between the APA and MLA styles, such as the order of the listing of first and last names of second (and third, etc.) authors when there is a work by more than one author.[18] As with the APA style, in the works-cited page, entries are indented after the first line.

Here is an example of the MLA style using the author page number for the citation:

"To begin with, nineteenth-century Europe helped to standardize the practice of fully *excluding* women from political authority around the world" (Towns 187).

Or

As Towns argues, "To begin with, nineteenth-century Europe helped to standardize the practice of fully *excluding* women from political authority around the world" (187).

Book with one author

(Towns 187)

For the works-cited list, the author's last name goes first (inverted: last name, first name, and then middle name if there is one), followed by the title of publication (italicized; all major words are capitalized, even in the subtitle), location of publication, name of publisher, date, and medium of publication. Note the period after the author's name. Also note that for university

---

[18] Turabian, *Student's Guide to Writing College Papers*, 186; *MLA Handbook for Writers of Research Papers*, xvii.

press, the abbreviation "UP" is listed (if it was the University of California Press, you would

write: U of California P).[19]

Towns, Ann E. *Women and States: Norms and Hierarchies in International Society*. New

      York: Cambridge UP, 2010. Print.

Book with two or three authors

(Ackerly and True 15)

For the works-cited list, the first author's name is listed by last name first (inverted: last name,

first name); the second (and third, if applicable) author's name is listed by first name and then

last name. Note the period after the last name of the last author listed. The title of the book

follows (italicized, with all major words capitalized), then the location of publication, the name

of the publisher, the date, and publication medium.[20]

Ackerly, Brooke, and Jaqui True. *Doing Feminist Research in Political and Social Science*. New

      York: Palgrave Macmillan, 2010. Print.

Book with four or more authors

(Spiegel, Matthews, Taw, and Williams 45)

For subsequent citations, one can use "et al."

---

[19] *MLA Handbook for Writers of Research Papers*, 128, 149.
[20] *MLA Handbook for Writers of Research Papers*, 154.

(Spiegel et al. 45)

For the works-cited page, if there are four or more authors, you can either write out the names of all the authors or use "et al." [21] Also note that in this example, the book is the fifth edition, which is indicated after the book title. Edition is abbreviated "ed."

Spiegel, Steven L., Elizabeth G. Matthews, Jennifer M. Taw, and Kristen P. Williams. *World Politics in a New Era*. 5th ed. New York: Oxford UP, 2012. Print.

or

Spiegel, Steven L., et al. *World Politics in a New Era*. 5th ed. New York: Oxford UP, 2012. Print.

An edited book

(Berger and Huntington)

As this is an edited book and the citation is for the entire book, the abbreviation (eds.) is placed after the names of the editors. In this case there are two editors, so write "eds." If there was only one editor, use "ed."

Berger, Peter L., and Samuel P. Huntington, eds. *Many Globalizations: Cultural Diversity in the Contemporary World*. New York: Oxford UP, 2002. Print.

---

[21] *MLA Handbook for Writers of Research Papers*, 215.

Chapter in an edited book

(Berger 14)

Note that in the works-cited list, the title of the chapter has quotation marks and the word "In" is not placed before the book title, as is the case with the APA style. In addition, the title of the book is followed by "Ed." and before the editors' names (use: "Ed." regardless of whether one or more editors, as the abbreviation "Ed." is for "edited by").

Berger, Peter L. "The Cultural Dynamics of Globalization." *Many Globalizations: Cultural Diversity in the Contemporary World.* Ed. Peter L. Berger and Samuel P. Huntington. Oxford: Oxford UP, 2002. 1–16. Print.

Journal article

(Ikenberry 57–58)

Quotation marks are placed around the title of the article. The journal title is italicized, followed by the volume number, a period, the issue number, date (in parentheses), colon, and the page range of the entire journal article, a period, followed by the publication medium.[22]

Ikenberry, G. John. "The Future of the Liberal World Order: Internationalism after America." *Foreign Affairs* 90.3 (2011): 56–68. Print.

---

[22] *MLA Handbook for Writers of Research Papers*, 137.

As a journal volume often has several issues each year, the issue number (as well as the month or

season) can be omitted "if the journal's pages are numbered continuously" for the entire

volume.[23] In other words, if volume 1 of a journal has three issues per year (volume 1, issue no.

1; volume 1, issue no. 2; volume 1, issue no. 3) and the pagination for the three issues is

continuous until the new volume (in this case, volume 2) is published, there is no need to include

the issue number. Thus, if the page numbers for volume 1, issue 1 range from 1 to 100, and

volume 1, issue 2 begins on page 101, the issue number can be omitted. If, however, each new

issue begins with page 1, you need to include the issue number (and month or season, if

applicable). Thus, if the page numbers for volume 1, issue 1 range from 1 to 100 and issue 2

starts on page 1 again, the issue number needs to be included on the works-cited page for that

entry.

Magazine article

(Di Giovanni 47)

For the works-cited page, if a magazine is published weekly or every two weeks, include the

date. The date includes the day and the month (all months but May, June, and July are

abbreviated). If the magazine is published monthly, bimonthly, or quarterly, indicate the month

and year of publication. In both cases, regardless of how often the magazine is published, the

volume and issue numbers of a magazine are not included. If the page numbers are not

consecutively listed, just indicate the number of the first page of the article and then add a plus

(+) sign to indicate that the article is longer than that one page. In the example below, *TIME*

---

[23] Gibaldi, *MLA Handbook for Writers of Research Papers*, 150.

magazine is published weekly, and so the full date is listed. Note the colon after the year and

before the page numbers.[24]

Di Giovanni, Janine. "The Making of a Monster." *TIME* 6 June 2011: 46–49. Print.

Newspaper article

(Gorman A4)

The headline of the article is in quotation marks, while the newspaper title is italicized; the date

is written as follows: day, month, year, followed by a colon and then the page number(s). As

with magazines, with the exception of May, June, and July, abbreviate the names of the months

(Jan.). Volume and issue numbers are not included. Make sure to include the publication

medium. Note too that in this example the word "The" is omitted from *The Wall Street Journal.*[25]

Gorman, Siobhan. "Cyberspies Target China Experts." *Wall Street Journal* 6 June 2011: A4.

     Print.

Internet source

(USAID)

In the works-cited page, list any author first, followed by the title of the work (italicized).

Indicate the date (day month year) after the title of the work. Also note that the publication

---

[24] *MLA Handbook for Writers of Research Papers*, 142-43.
[25] *MLA Handbook for Writers of Research Papers*, 141.

medium is listed as Web. The access (or retrieval) date follows and is written before the URL.

Angle brackets < > are inserted on either side of the URL. The *MLA Handbook* also recognizes

that URLs change or become inactive. If that is the case, you can omit the URL as long as the

information you do provide is sufficient enough that the source can be found.[26]

U.S. Agency for International Development. *Conflict Mitigation and Prevention.* 17 May 2013.

      Web. 23 May 2013. <http://www.usaid.gov/what-we-do/working-crises-and-

      conflict/conflict-mitigation-and-prevention>

Other things to keep in mind when you cite and write using the MLA style:

- If an author has the same last name as another author, you will need to indicate in the in-
  text citation the different authors by using the first initial and last name and the page
  number: (V. S. Peterson 50) and (J. Peterson 31).[27]

- If you are citing more than one work from the same author published in the same year,
  you will need to differentiate the publications by including a short title in the citation that
  is italicized, followed by the page number (Peterson, *Feminist Theories* 35).[28]

- If you are citing more than one work from the same author (regardless of whether these
  works were published in the same year), you need to list them in the works-cited page,
  listing the titles of the works alphabetically. Write the author's full name on the first entry

---

[26] *MLA Handbook for Writers of Research Papers*, 181-82
[27] *MLA Handbook for Writers of Research Papers*, 215.
[28] *MLA Handbook for Writers of Research Papers*, 127.

only, followed by 3-em dashes for the author's name for the subsequent entries.[29] For

example:

Singer, David J. "International Conflict: Three Levels of Analysis." *World Politics* 12.3 (April

1960): 453–61.

---. "The Level-of-Analysis Program in International Relations." *World Politics* 14.1

(October 1961): 77–92.

- If you are citing several authors in the same citation, you will need to write all the

  authors' last names, followed by the page number. The authors are listed alphabetically

  by last name, and each author's entry is separated by a semicolon (Peterson 50; Singer

  453).[30]

Chicago Style: Citations and Bibliography

For the Chicago style, there are two acceptable forms: the parenthetical author-date

reference and the notes system (footnotes and endnotes).

Author-date system[31]

In terms of the parenthetical author-date system, the Chicago style includes only the

author and the date of publication (that is why it is called the "author-date" system). If a page

number is included, it follows the date and a comma (Smith 2011, 5). There is no comma after

---

[29] *MLA Handbook for Writers of Research Papers*, 133-34; Turabian, *Student's Guide to Writing College Papers*, 188.

[30] *MLA Handbook for Writers of Research Papers*, 229.

[31] See *The Chicago Manual of Style: The Essential Guide for Writers, Editors, and Publishers*, 16th ed. (Chicago: University of Chicago Press, 2010), chapter 15, for more specifics on the Chicago author-date system.

the author's last name. For the references page, the second and subsequent lines of the entry are indented (you can use the "tab" function on your word processor).[32] Also note that the important words in the titles are capitalized.

Book with one author

(Towns 2010, 25)

In the references page entry the author's last name comes first, followed by the first name (or any initials), period, date of publication, period, title of book (in italics), period, location of publisher, colon, name of publisher, period.[33]

Towns, Ann E. 2010. *Women and States: Norms and Hierarchies in International Society*. New York: Cambridge University Press.

Book with two or three authors

(Ackerly and True 2010)

For the references page, only the first author's last name goes first. The second (and third if applicable) author's name is listed as first name and then last name. The word "and" is placed before the last author's name. The rest of the required information (and punctuation) follows that of the book with a single author.[34]

---

[32] *The Chicago Manual of Style*, 789.
[33] *The Chicago Manual of Style*, 790.
[34] *The Chicago Manual of Style*, 790.

Ackerly, Brooke, and Jacqui True. 2010. *Doing Feminist Research in Political and Social*

    Science. New York: Palgrave Macmillan.

Book with four or more authors

(Spiegel et al. 2012)

For the references page, all authors' names are listed, again with the first author's name inverted

(last name first), with the word "and" placed before the last author's name, and the rest of the

bibliographic information and punctuation follows the same format as that for single-author

books.[35]

Spiegel, Steven L., Elizabeth G. Matthews, Jennifer M. Taw, and Kristen P. Williams. 2012.

    World Politics in a New Era, 5th ed. New York: Oxford University Press.

An edited book

(Berger and Huntington 2002)

Do not include "ed." (for "editor") in the in-text citation. In the references entry, however, do

indicate the editor. If there is only one editor, use "ed." If there is more than one editor, use

"eds."[36]

---

[35] *The Chicago Manual of Style*, 790-91.
[36] *The Chicago Manual of Style*, 790.

Berger, Peter L., and Samuel P. Huntington, eds. 2002. *Many Globalizations: Cultural Diversity

in the Contemporary World*. New York: Oxford University Press.

Chapter in an edited book

(Berger 2002, 12)

For the references entry, the author of the chapter's name is listed (last name first). The title of

the chapter is placed within quotation marks. The title of the book is italicized, and the word "In"

is placed before the title of the book. After the title of the book, write "edited by" and then the

names of the editors (first name, last name). The page numbers for the entire chapter are listed,

separated by a comma from the name(s) of the editor(s). The location of the publisher, colon, and

name of publisher follows.[37]

Berger, Peter L. 2002. "The Cultural Dynamics of Globalization." In *Many Globalizations:

Cultural Diversity in the Contemporary World*, edited by Peter L. Berger and Samuel P.

Huntington, 1–16. Oxford: Oxford University Press.

Journal article

(Ikenberry 2011, 57)

For the references entry, quotation marks bracket the title of the article. The title of the journal is

italicized. The volume and issue numbers are given (the issue number is set inside parentheses).

---

[37] *The Chicago Manual of Style*, 791.

If there is a month or season, it can be inserted in place of the issue number (in parentheses).

Place a colon after the issue number, followed by the page range of the article.[38]

Ikenberry, G. John. 2011. "The Future of the Liberal World Order: Internationalism after

America." *Foreign Affairs* 90 (3): 56–68.

Magazine article

(Di Giovanni 2011)

Note in the references entry, the author's name goes first (period), year (period), followed by the

title of the article in quotation marks. The name of the magazine is in italics. The month and day

(comma) are followed by the page range of the article.[39]

Di Giovanni, Janine. 2011. "The Making of a Monster." *TIME,* June 6, 46–49.

Newspaper article

(Gorman 2011)

Note that the year of publication and the month and day are separated in the references entry.

The headline is in quotations, and the name of the newspaper is italicized. Commas are used after

the name of the newspaper and the date (also note that in this example the word "The" is omitted

from "The Wall Street Journal").

---

[38] *The Chicago Manual of Style*, 791.
[39] *The Chicago Manual of Style*, 807

Gorman, Siobhan. 2011. "Cyberspies Target China Experts." *Wall Street Journal*, June 6,

    A4.

Internet source

(USAID 2013)

In the references page, if there is no date for the source, you can include the accessed by/retrieval

date. The year follows the author's name, and placed before the title (which is in quotation

marks). The month and day are written before the URL. Use a period after the URL.[40]

U.S. Agency for International Development. 2013. "Conflict Mitigation and Prevention."

    Accessed May 23. http://www.usaid.gov/what-we-do/working-crises-and-

    conflict/conflict-mitigation-and-prevention.

Notes: footnotes and endnotes[41]

    Many scholars and publishers use the notes system rather than the in-text citation system

as it allows for better flow for the reader. The flow of a sentence is not interrupted by a citation

(Smith 2011) in the middle. In addition, authors can include information or additional

commentary in the note (a "substantive note") that may not be essential in the body of the paper

itself but provides the reader with additional information.

---

[40] *The Chicago Manual of Style*, 808.
[41] Refer to *The Chicago Manual of Style*, chapter 14, for more specifics on the Chicago note system. Also see chapter 18 in Turabian, *Student's Guide to Writing College Papers*, for discussion of the Chicago style.

The only difference between a footnote and an endnote is the placement of the note. For footnotes, the information is found at the bottom of the page (the "footer"), whereas for endnotes, the information is found at the end of the paper.[42] In both cases, you need to insert the note number at the end of the sentence or paragraph you are citing. Your word processor should have a footnote/endnote function. Make sure that you have indicated that the numbers are to be inserted consecutively, starting on page 1 of your paper (or wherever in the paper the first note is needed). Use Arabic numerals (1, 2, 3 . . .), not lowercase Roman numerals (i, ii, iii . . .) or lowercase alphabet (a, b, c . . .). The superscript, as the note number is called, goes outside the punctuation marks. For example, the note number is placed outside the quotation mark and the period in the following sentence:

> Ackerly and True state that "A fundamental concern of feminist researchers across a range of social science subjects is the study of power and its effects."[1]

The note is written as follows (the first line is indented but subsequent lines are flush to the left margin):

> 1. Brooke Ackerly and Jacqui True, *Doing Feminist Research in Political and Social Science* (New York: Palgrave Macmillan, 2010), 21.

For the actual size of the note number in the footnote, it is usually a superscript, but for an endnote, it is the same size font as the text. See the comparison of the note number (1) for the footnote and endnote:

---

[42] *The Chicago Manual of Style*, 671-73.

Footnote:

[1] Brooke Ackerly and Jacqui True, *Doing Feminist Research in Political and Social Science* (New York: Palgrave Macmillan, 2010), 21.

Endnote:

1. Brooke Ackerly and Jacqui True, *Doing Feminist Research in Political and Social Science* (New York: Palgrave Macmillan, 2010), 21.

For both footnotes and endnotes, the author's first name is listed first, followed by the last name (in the bibliography, the last name goes first as authors are listed alphabetically by last name). Commas are used to separate author, title, and page numbers in the notes. Additionally, once the first citation is noted, subsequent same works can be inserted as the "short form" (usually the author's last name, title of publication [journal article, book title, or chapter title], and page number [if applicable]).[43] Using the example above, if note number 2 refers to the same source, the short form is written as follows:

2. Ackerly and True, *Doing Feminist Research*, 24.

Book with one author

Note that in the footnote/endnote, after the author's name and the title of the publication, the publisher location (colon), publisher's name (comma), and date are enclosed with parentheses, followed by a comma and then the page number.[44]

---

[43] *The Chicago Manual of Style*, 660-61, 667-68.
[44] *The Chicago Manual of Style*, 661-62.

1. Ann E. Towns, *Women and States: Norms and Hierarchies in International Society* (New York: Cambridge University Press, 2010), 35.

For the bibliography, the author's last name is first, followed by the first name. A period follows the author's first name (or initial, if applicable). The title of the book is italicized, followed by a period. The location of the publisher is followed by a colon (:), followed by the name of the publisher, followed by a comma (,) and then the date of publication (copyright date). The publication information is not bracketed by parentheses.[45]

Towns, Ann E. *Women and States: Norms and Hierarchies in International Society*. New
         York: Cambridge University Press, 2010.

Book with two or three authors

1. Brooke Ackerly, and Jacqui True, *Doing Feminist Research in Political and Social Science* (New York: Palgrave Macmillan, 2010), 21.

For the bibliography the first author's last name is placed first, and the second (or third if applicable) author's name is first name first, followed by the last name.[46]

Ackerly, Brooke, and Jacqui True. *Doing Feminist Research in Political and Social Science*.
         New York: Palgrave Macmillan, 2010.

---

[45] *The Chicago Manual of Style*, 661-62.
[46] *The Chicago Manual of Style*, 663.

Book with four or more authors

For the citation, with four or more authors, include only the first author's name, followed by "et al."[47] Note that there is a period after "al" followed by a comma. As this is the fifth edition of the book, the edition information follows the title of the book and is abbreviated "ed."

     1. Steven L. Spiegel, et al., *World Politics in a New Era*, 5th ed. (New York: Oxford University Press, 2012), 225.

For the bibliography, the first author's name is listed (last name first) and followed by the other authors (first name, last name) in the order in which they appear on the title page of the book. All the authors must be listed in the bibliographic entry.[48]

Spiegel, Steven L., Elizabeth G. Matthews, Jennifer M. Taw, and Kristen P. Williams. *World*
     Politics in a New Era, 5th ed. New York: Oxford University Press, 2012.

Edited Book

For the citation, the word "editor(s)" is abbreviated: ed. (or eds. if there is more than one editor). With more than one editor, use the word "and" and not an ampersand (&) between the editors' names.[49]

---

[47] *The Chicago Manual of Style*, 663.
[48] *The Chicago Manual of Style*, 663.
[49] *The Chicago Manual of Style*, 695.

1. Peter L. Berger and Samuel P. Huntington, eds., *Many Globalizations: Cultural Diversity in the Contemporary World* (Oxford: Oxford University Press, 2002).

For the bibliography, the editor (or first editors') last name is first, followed by "ed." to indicate it is an edited book. Again, the second editor's name appears as first name followed by last name.

Berger, Peter. L., and Samuel P. Huntington, eds. *Many Globalizations: Cultural Diversity in the Contemporary World*. Oxford: Oxford University Press, 2002.

Chapter in edited book

For the note citation, the title of the chapter is in quotation marks. The word "in" (lower case) is placed after the title of the chapter and before the title of the book (which is italicized). The abbreviation for editor, "ed." or "eds.," is placed after the title of the book, and then the names of the editor(s).[50]

1. Peter L. Berger, "The Cultural Dynamics of Globalization," in *Many Globalizations: Cultural Diversity in the Contemporary World*, eds. Peter L. Berger and Samuel P. Huntington (Oxford: Oxford University Press, 2002), 15.

---

[50] *The Chicago Manual of Style*, 664.

For the bibliographic entry, the word "In" (capitalized) is placed before the title of the book. The phrase "edited by" follows the title of the book and appears before the names of the editor(s). The names of the editors are listed (first name, last name), followed by the page range of the chapter, and then a period. The publisher's information is then listed.[51]

Berger, Peter L. "The Cultural Dynamics of Globalization." In *Many Globalizations: Cultural Diversity in the Contemporary World*, edited by Peter L. Berger and Samuel P. Huntington, 1–16. Oxford: Oxford University Press, 2002.

Journal article

For a journal article, the title of the article is enclosed in quotation marks, and the title of the journal is in italics, followed by the volume and issue number, and the relevant page numbers follow the colon. The issue number can be omitted if there is a month or a season. Note the use of commas in the citation, and the periods in the bibliographic entry. In the bibliographic entry, the entire page range of the article is listed. [52]

1. G. John Ikenberry, "The Future of the Liberal World Order: Internationalism after America," *Foreign Affairs* 90, 3 (May/June 2011): 58.

Ikenberry, G. John. "The Future of the Liberal World Order: Internationalism after America." *Foreign Affairs* 90, 3 (May/June 2011): 56–68.

---

[51] *The Chicago Manual of Style*, 665, 707.
[52] *The Chicago Manual of Style*, 664, 729-32.

Magazine article

For magazines, the volume and issue number are not included in either the note or the

bibliographic entry. For the bibliographic entry, because magazine articles are often not

consecutively printed (there might be a one-page advertisement within the article for example),

the page numbers can be omitted.[53]

1. Janine Di Giovanni, "The Making of a Monster." *TIME*, June 6, 2011, 48.

Di Giovanni, Janine. "The Making of a Monster." *TIME,* June 6, 2011.

Newspaper article

For a newspaper article, put quotation marks around the headline, italicize the newspaper name

(note that in this example "The" has been omitted for the *The Wall Street Journal*), followed by

the month, day and year. Page numbers can be omitted, given that there are sometimes different

editions of the same newspaper on the same day.[54]

1. Siobhan Gorman, "Cyberspies Target China Experts," *Wall Street Journal*, June 6,

2001, A4.

Gorman, Siobhan. "Cyberspies Target China Experts." *Wall Street Journal*, June 6, 2001,

A4.

---

[53] *The Chicago Manual of Style*, 729.
[54] *The Chicago Manual of Style*, 739-40.

<u>Internet source</u>

For an internet source, include the author and the document title (in quotation marks), followed by the title of the website, date of publication (if available) and accessed date (definitely include an accessed date if there's no date of publication), and then the URL or DOI.[55] In the citation, a comma is used after the accessed date and before the URL or DOI, while in the bibliography, the accessed date is followed by a period.

1. U.S. Agency for International Development, "Conflict Mitigation and Prevention," accessed May 23, 2013, http://www.usaid.gov/what-we-do/working-crises-and-conflict/conflict-mitigation-and-prevention.

U.S. Agency for International Development. "Conflict Mitigation and Prevention." Accessed May 23, 2013. http://www.usaid.gov/what-we-do/working-crises-and-conflict/conflict-mitigation-and-prevention.

Other things to keep in mind when you cite and write using the Chicago style:

- If you are citing more than one work from the same author (regardless of whether these works were published in the same year), you need to list them in the bibliography. If they were published in different years, list them chronologically from the oldest to the most recent. Write the author's full name on the first entry only, followed by 3-em dashes for the author's name for the subsequent entries.[56] For example:

---

[55] *The Chicago Manual of Style*, 733-34, 752-53.
[56] *The Chicago Manual of Style*, 691-92.

Singer, David J. "International Conflict: Three Levels of Analysis." *World Politics* 12, 3 (April

1960): 453–61.

---. "The Level-of-Analysis Program in International Relations." *World Politics* 14, 1

(October 1961): 77–92.

- As was noted earlier, after the first time you cite an author, you can use the short form for

  subsequent citations (name, title of work, and page number). Since you might be citing

  more than one work by the same author, including the title of the work enables you to

  indicate which work is being cited. Using the Singer example above, after the first full

  citation (say, note number 1), for the next citation you would write:

3. Singer, "International Conflict."

If note number 2 referred to Singer's second article, with the full citation indicated, any

subsequent citation referring to that work would be written as:

5. Singer, "The Level-of-Analysis Problem."

Thus, the reader knows that note number 3 refers to the "International Conflict" article published

in 1960 and note number 5 refers to "The Level-of-Analysis Problem" article published in 1961.

- Authors also use "Ibid." (an abbreviation for "ibidem," which in Latin means "in the

  same place"). Ibid is used in a footnote or endnote to refer to the work in the immediately previous citation. Thus, if you cited Peterson in note 1 and then cited the same work in note 2, you could write: Ibid. If all the information is the same in both notes (author, title of work, page number, etc.), you can write just: Ibid. If, however, the information is the same except for different page numbers, you write: Ibid., followed by the page number.[57] Ibid. can be used only for a single citation, not when you have multiple citations in the same note, unless all the citations in the previous note are also in the subsequent note.

A word of caution in using Ibid. Because it is easy to move sentences and paragraphs around with the "cut and paste" functions on word processors, notes can be easily moved too and then be out of place. You need to make sure that the Ibid. does indeed follow the note before it. For example, if note 1 is Peterson, "Feminist Theories"; note 2 is Singer, "Level-of-Analysis"; and note 3 is Ibid., then Ibid. refers to the Singer citation in note 2. If you move the information for note 3 (and the note itself) to follow the Peterson citation (note 1), the reader will assume that the Ibid. (new note 2) refers to Peterson (note 1) and not Singer. In addition, Singer note 2 has now become note 3 because the word processor will automatically renumber the notes to reflect the "cut and paste" action—that you moved information, including the note. By moving the information and note 3 to follow note 1, you will need to correct the new note 2, replacing the word "Ibid." with: Singer, "Level-of-Analysis."

- If you are using the Chicago author-date system and you have two citations for the same year by the same author, you need to use a, b, c, and so on, to differentiate the various sources.[58] For example, V. Spike Peterson had two pieces published in 2004:

---

[57] *The Chicago Manual of Style*, 669.
[58] *The Chicago Manual of Style*, 795.

Peterson, V. Spike. "Feminist Theories Within, Invisible to, and Beyond IR." *Brown*

Journal of World Affairs X, 2 (Winter/Spring 2004): 35–46.

Peterson, V. Spike. "Plural Processes, Patterned Connections." *Globalizations* 1, 1

(September 2004): 50–68.

In using the author-date system, if you write only (Peterson 2004), the reader cannot tell which

of the two works is being cited. Thus, in the in-text citation, you would write:

(Peterson 2004a)

This would refer to the article, "Feminist Theories Within." Writing (Peterson 2004b) would

refer to the article "Plural Processes." The bibliographic entry would then list the "a" and "b"

next to the year so that the reader would know which work is being cited.

Peterson, V. Spike. "Feminist Theories Within, Invisible to, and Beyond IR." *Brown*

Journal of World Affairs X, 2 (Winter/Spring 2004a): 35–46.

Peterson, V. Spike. "Plural Processes, Patterned Connections." *Globalizations* 1, 1

(September 2004b): 50–68.

E-BOOKS: Tushar Rae, "E-Books' Varied Formats Makes Citations a Mess for Scholars," February 6, 2011, accessed May 9, 2011, http://chronicle.com/article/E-Books-Varied-Formats-Make/126246/.

As e-reading devices gain popularity, professors and students are struggling to adapt them to an academic fundamental: proper citations, which other scholars can use.

The trouble is that in electronic formats, there are no fixed pages. The Kindle, developed by Amazon, does away with page numbers entirely. Along with other e-book readers, the Kindle allows users to change font style and size, so the number of words on a screen can vary. Instead of pages, it uses "location numbers" that relate to a specific part of a book.

Other devices, like the Sony Reader, which reflows text based on font size and model of device, have different methods, so the same passage might have a different identifier. Things get more confusing when readers come in various screen sizes.

The inability to find passages limits scholarly research, academics complain, because they depend on citations not only to track down and analyze text, but also as a testament to the accuracy of their own work. "The lack of page numbers is disconcerting," says Rosemary G. Feal, executive director of the Modern Language Association.

To provide guidance for the e-book world, the three major keepers of academic-citation style—the Modern Language Association's *MLA Handbook for Writers of Research Papers,* the American Psychological Association, and the University of Chicago Press, publisher of *The Chicago Manual of Style*—have taken steps to answer the question of how to cite e-books. But many scholars are unaware of such guidelines, or find the new citation styles awkward.

The MLA suggests treating all e-books in the same way as a digital file (like a Microsoft Word document posted online) when listed in a bibliography. That means simply adding the kind of digital file used to the end of the traditional citation. To indicate where the snippet comes from within the file, the MLA recommends using section and paragraph numbers, if available. That's the same way the handbook suggests handling any work that lacks page numbers.

Ms. Feal says the MLA is considering whether to "accommodate" location numbers on the Kindle.

The latest edition of the Chicago manual, released in 2010, suggests the use of section and paragraph numbers, along with section titles, if page numbers are not available. Another alternative: listing the chapter name or heading over a section of text, or even writing a short, searchable string of text in the citation to help users find it.

"In desperation, you could say, 'Near the reference to "fuzzy rabbits,"' or something that would maybe be unique in the book," suggests Carol F. Saller, senior manuscript editor and assistant managing editor of the books division at the Chicago Press. "I wouldn't recommend that as a first tactic."

The Chicago manual also suggests including the format or edition of an e-book when listing it on a reference list.

For example, according to the manual's Web site, a copy of Jane Austen's *Pride and Prejudice* accessed on a Kindle might be cited as: "Jane Austen, *Pride and Prejudice* (New York: Penguin Classics, 2007), Kindle edition."

New Technology, New Rules

The keepers of official citation style can find it tough to decide which new technologies need special rules.

The staying power of a new digital-book platform or online service is unpredictable, Ms. Saller says, so the Chicago editors struggle with whether to craft guidelines for specific systems. When they started drafting the latest edition of their style manual, three years ago, they decided not to include Twitter-specific citation rules, because they were not sure if the medium would survive. Since then they have received numerous questions, mostly from high-school and college students, about how to cite tweets.

Many scholars remain unaware that major guidebooks have added rules for e-books at all. "I don't think people have absorbed the fact that we have addressed the issue," says Ms. Saller. The American Psychology Association's guidebook, like Chicago's, suggests listing section and paragraph numbers or section titles when quoting e-books that lack page numbers.

"It is a little unwieldy, but it's the best option we have been able to come up with that transfers across platforms to get the reader back to the source the writer used," says Jeff Hume-Pratuch, an editorial supervisor at the APA.

Scholars who are familiar with such citations agree that the current formats remain unwieldy. Some academics improvise to help alleviate that burden.

Joseph Reagle, a fellow at Harvard University's Berkman Center for Internet & Society and author of *Good Faith Collaboration: The Culture of Wikipedia*, has worked with e-books in researching the Internet communities he writes about.

"I struggled with it a lot as I was doing the scholarship myself and thought, 'I don't want to put anyone else through this,'" he says.
When Mr. Reagle published *Good Faith Collaboration* online, he numbered the sections and paragraphs of each chapter to help anyone who wanted to cite the digital text.

Catching On at Colleges

While those numbers may be effective landmarks, some fear that they may start to intrude on the text. "What I don't want is something that so gums up the whole text that I can't pay attention to the text anymore," says William Rankin, director of educational innovation and an associate professor of English at Abilene Christian University, which is experimenting with e-books in some courses.

"What I want is something that lets me find something when I need to but also gets out of the way and lets me read."

Roberto Tietzmann, a professor of film at the Pontifical Catholic University of Rio Grande do Sul, in Brazil, cites Kindle books by inserting an "l," for location number, where the "p" of the page number usually is found, and using footnotes to explain what the "l" stands for.

He uses e-books often, he says, because Brazilian publishers typically "release e-books more quickly than paper books." It is also easier to access an e-book than to wait for a paper version to arrive from the United States or elsewhere, he adds.

"E-books are under debate, and meanwhile these rules are not stabilized—I adapted them out of common sense and previous rules," he says via e-mail.

Discussions of how to cite e-books, which have been heating up on some academic e-mail lists and in faculty lounges, appear to be evidence that the format is catching on at colleges.

"I think digital books will be the main kinds of books teachers and students will be using," says Mr. Rankin, predicting that in about five years, there will be firm rules for citing e-books.

He looks forward to a time when most reading is done digitally, and electronic links replace long descriptions of how to find each reference.

"Citations have always been symbolic," Mr. Rankin says. "I don't think I need symbolic anymore. I want an actual link."

CONCLUSION

This chapter has presented you with the three main citation styles (citations and bibliographic entries) used in academic research and writing. Whichever style you use (or are required to use by your professor), you must be consistent. You cannot make up your own style as there are conventions about the proper citation format; that includes whether titles are italicized or there are quotation marks and so forth. Finally, the key point to take away from this chapter is the importance of documenting one's research and attributing the research done by others to give them credit for the work they have done. The mantra to remember is: Cite, cite, and cite some more!

Chapter 5

Conclusion—Further Readings

As you now know, all scholars begin with a research question, or puzzle. They then conduct an extensive search for the relevant literature on their topic, evaluating and analyzing the research done by others. The process of gathering research enables one to find what answers to the question have already been provided, where gaps in the literature remain, and how one's research can fill those gaps. This book—a short primer—has provided you with the basic tools to conduct research and write a research paper in political science. You now know how to think of a research question and construct a hypothesis and gather the relevant research. You know how to organize a research paper because you know the parts of a paper. You know what needs to be included to present a coherent and effective piece of writing.

Libraries and an assortment of online databases are invaluable resources for your project. Libraries and librarians remain important repositories for legitimate and credible sources. Librarians have the skills and expertise to navigate through the vast amount of information available for researchers. At the same time, the World Wide Web offers a huge amount of information, but you have learned how to be a smart consumer of the information found on the Internet.

You are also informed about the need to cite the works of others; their contributions to building knowledge need to be acknowledged and recognized. The construction of new knowledge is built on the knowledge of others. You have learned to take notes effectively and organize your research notes to help you write an effective paper.

Writing the research paper poses its own set of challenges. It is often hard to get started writing, and it is easy to research more and more. Seeing the blank page on the computer screen can lead to a sense of frustration and fear. But as you have found, we hope, in this book, researching and writing a paper can be a very exciting and rewarding experience.

By way of conclusion, for additional sources on writing and research, the following is a list of books for political science papers specifically, followed by a list of general books on writing research papers.

Books for political science papers:

Ackerly, Brooke, and Jacqui True. *Doing Feminist Research in Political and Social Science.* **New York: Palgrave Macmillan, 2010. [303 pp]**

This book proffers "a critical feminist perspective" that is "focused on how to do feminist research" (p. 1). Although this is definitely an advanced text, undergraduates will find it useful for its very detailed discussion of the research and writing process from a feminist perspective, utilizing gender analysis. Chapter topics include formulating a good research question, developing theory and the literature review, research design, data collection (i.e., interviews, surveys, focus groups), and writing and publishing. Examples from feminist research are provided throughout.

American Political Science Association, *Style Manual for Political Science***, revised edition. Washington, DC: American Political Science Association, 2001. [45 pp]**

Prepared by the American Political Science Association (APSA) as a guide for submission of articles to the *American Political Science Review* (APSR) journal, the manual covers various topics, including title, abstract, length, headings, acronyms and abbreviations, gender-neutral language, and equations and variables. The citation section provides examples on chronology, multiple authors and works, government documents, and electronic sources. The notes section gives examples of interviews and personal communications and newspaper articles, and the references section covers books (one author, multiple authors, edited volumes, chapter in a multiauthor work), journal articles, unpublished works, and government documents. According to the guide, "In matters of editorial style, APSA follows the latest edition of the Chicago Manual of Style (CMS)" (p. 9).

Baglione, Lisa A. *Writing a Research Paper in Political Science: A Practical Guide to Inquiry, Structure, and Methods*. Belmont, CA: Thomson Wadsworth, 2007. [184 pp] The book provides a clear and concise discussion of the various parts of a research paper specifically for political science. Chapters are devoted to a research paper's constituent parts: finding a research question (Chapter 2), literature review (Chapter 3), thesis/model/hypothesis (Chapter 4), introduction (Chapter 5), research design (Chapter 6), evaluating the argument (Chapter 7), conclusion (Chapter 8), and revising/editing (Chapter 9). Each chapter uses hypothetical examples introduced in the first chapter and then applied throughout the remaining chapters; and each also has a "Practical Summary," "Suggested Calendar," and "Exercises." Some chapters have a "Checklist" at the end.

Carlson, James M., and Mark S. Hyde. *Doing Empirical Political Research*. Boston: Houghton Mifflin Co., 2003. [436 pp exclusive of appendix, glossary, and index]

In four parts and 18 chapters, *Doing Empirical Political Research* is focused on research methods ("scientific method") specifically for undergraduate political science majors. The book covers topics such as developing a research question, formulating a hypothesis, finding sources, doing literature reviews, and presenting data/results. As the book is predominantly focused on the scientific method, chapters also address topics such as causality (Chapter 6), "Conceptualizing, Operationalizing, and Measuring Variables" (Chapter. 7), collecting data, using surveys, the case study approach, and "Determining the Statistical Significance of Results" (Chapter 17). Each chapter ends with several activities related to that chapter's main topic.

Charlton, Lucille, and Mark Charlton. *Thomson Nelson Guide to Research and Writing in Political Science*. **Toronto: Nelson, 2006. [95 pp inclusive of appendix]**

This relatively short but clear guide is very concise. It begins with a discussion of the research process, which includes evaluating primary and secondary sources and using the Internet. Chapter 2 offers useful suggestions for gathering and organizing information, such as note taking and creating a working bibliography. Subsequent chapters focus on different types of writing assignments, including a research essay, briefing papers, op-ed articles, policy analysis papers, and a literature review. The book also covers citation formats (APA, MLA, and Chicago) and writing styles (i.e., punctuation).

Roselle, Laura, and Sharon Spray. *Research and Writing in International Relations*. **New York: Pearson Longman, 2008. [162 pp]**

Focused on the international relations (IR) subfield within political science, this book is divided into three parts. Part I covers the basic steps for researching and writing a paper (selecting a topic and formulating a research question, finding scholarly sources and writing a literature review, research design, writing parts of the paper). The four chapters in Part II, "Project Resources," each provide a general research question followed by suggested resources for particular topics (and subtopics within each chapter) in international relations: "International Conflict and Military Force" (Chapter 5), "Foreign Policy" (Chapter 6), "International Cooperation and International Law" (Chapter 7), and "International Political Economy, Globalization, and Development" (Chapter 8). The three chapters in Part III, "Writing Resources," discuss finding and organizing research (i.e., note taking), citing sources, and style guidelines (i.e., gender-neutral language, newspaper titles).

Schmidt, Diane E. *Writing in Political Science: A Practical Guide*, **4th edition. New York: Pearson Longman, 2010. [400 pp]**

Writing in Political Science is a very detailed and comprehensive step-by-step instruction for finding a topic, finding useful sources, using quantitative and qualitative research, and writing the parts of an essay and research paper (thesis sentence, paragraph, topic sentence). Chapters also cover "Common Writing Problems" such as stylistic errors and writer's block, formatting, and reference styles. Chapters 9 through 12 cover formatting and provide examples of several types of student assignments, including analytical essays, essay exams, annotated bibliographies, book reviews, research proposals, PowerPoint presentations, position papers, policy memos, grants, and research papers.

Scott, Gregory M., and Stephen M. Garrison. *The Political Science Student Writer's Manual*, **7th edition. New York: Pearson Longman, 2012. [197 pp]**

Divided into four parts and 14 chapters, this comprehensive manual provides students with an examination of political science as a field of study as well as serving as a guide for writing and researching different kinds of papers. Part I focuses on topics such as writing style (e.g., gender-neutral wording, capitalization, use of commas), formatting a paper, and citing sources. Part II discusses writing as a form of communication and how to go about writing political blogs, op-ed pieces, and book reviews. The research process is covered in Part III (for example, developing a bibliography and writing a literature review), and Part IV gives detailed instructions on how to write policy analysis papers, papers comparing political systems, amicus curiae briefs, and papers analyzing public opinion surveys.

Van Evera, Stephen. *Guide to Methods for Students of Political Science*. Ithaca, NY: Cornell University Press, 1997. [136 pp]

Primarily for graduate students in political science (it specifically "reflects" the author's "field of concentration [international relations/security affairs]"), as Chapters 3, 4, and 5 ("What Is a Political Science Dissertation?" "Helpful Hints on Writing a Political Science Dissertation," and "The Dissertation Proposal," respectively) indicate, this book offers helpful guidance to undergraduate students as well. Chapter 1 defines terms (theory, hypotheses, laws, and variables) and discusses how to test theories, and Chapter 2 discusses the use of the case-study method of research. The short appendix, "How to Write a Paper," provides very good (short and crisp) advice for undergraduate papers.

General books on research and writing papers:

Booth, Wayne G., Gregory G. Colomb, and Joseph M. Williams. *The Craft of Research*, **3rd edition. Chicago: University of Chicago Press, 2008. [317 pp]**

In five parts and 17 chapters, the book provides material for writing and researching, covering not just academic papers but also reports by those in government and business. The book begins with answering questions such as "What Is Research?" and "Why Write It Up?" The authors then make the point that one is writing for an audience of readers. Part II addresses the process of going from choosing a topic, to developing a research question, to finding sources. Part III, "Making a Claim and Supporting It," focuses on making a good argument, making claims, finding evidence, considering alternatives to one's argument, and warrants. Part IV, "Planning, Drafting, and Revising," details the drafting and revising processes and the use of visual aids (graphs, charts, etc), as well as how to structure the introduction and conclusion. Part V addresses "The Ethics of Research" and a "Postscript for Teachers." Many of the substantive chapters include a section at the end, "Quick Tips," for easy reference.

The Chicago Manual of Style, **16th edition. Chicago: University of Chicago Press, 2010. [1,026 pp]**

As the subtitle of this manual, "The Essential Guide for Writers, Editors, and Publishers," indicates, this is the "go-to" reference source for those using the "Chicago style." In addition to descriptions and examples of the citation style, the manual provides comprehensive and detailed coverage of all parts of a work to be published, including books and journals as well as web-based publications. Part I is focused on "The Publishing Process" (i.e., preparing, editing, and proofreading the manuscript; illustrations and tables; rights and permissions). Part II, "Style and

Usage," covers grammar, punctuation, spelling, names, numbers, abbreviations, foreign

languages, and quotations, and Part III is focused on documentation/citations (notes,

bibliography, and citation styles).

Kane, Thomas S. *The Oxford Essential Guide to Writing.* **New York: Berkley Books, 2000.**

[451 pp]

Based on *The Oxford Guide to Writing: A Rhetoric and Handbook for College Students*, the book

provides detailed descriptions on the writing process, how to structure an essay (beginning,

closing, end; expository paragraph; sentence structure), and grammar (diction, description and

narration, and punctuation). The goal of the book is to help the reader write effectively and

clearly. Most chapters end with a "For Practice" exercise related to the particular chapter's topic.

Lipson, Charles. *How to Write a BA Thesis: A Practical Guide from Your First Ideas to Your*

Finished Paper. **Chicago: University of Chicago Press, 2005. [402 pp]**

Focused on writing and researching a BA thesis, the book provides a suggested monthly timeline

for writers for the process of such a project. Lipson begins by discussing how to go about finding

a thesis topic and an advisor, followed by the research process (taking effective notes, avoiding

plagiarism, thesis proposal and background reading for the proposal, conducting the research,

use of case studies, developing a thesis statement/argument) and the writing process

("prewriting," writing, editing, "presenting information visually"). The book then discusses ways

to work efficiently and deal with problems that may arise as the thesis process continues. There

are chapters on frequently asked questions and the thesis defense. Each chapter provides a

checklist. Lipson also provides an appendix on sample citation styles (MLA, APA, Chicago).

MLA Handbook for Writers of Research Papers, **7th edition. New York: The Modern Language Association of America, 2009. [292 pp inclusive of appendix]**

Published by the Modern Language Association (MLA), the handbook begins with the specifics for the research and writing process (topic selection, conducting research, developing a working bibliography, evaluating sources, note taking, outlines, and drafts). Chapter 2, "Plagiarism and Academic Integrity," addresses plagiarism and when documentation is needed. Chapter 3, "The Mechanics of Writing," addresses grammar and spelling, and Chapter 43 covers the formatting of a research paper (margins, spacing, headings, etc.). The next two chapters (Chapters 5 and 6) provide detailed examples of the MLA style for citations within a paper and the works-cited page. The last chapter (Chapter 7) covers abbreviations. Sources by field and examples of citation formats other than MLA are found in the appendixes.

Strunk, William, Jr., and E. B. White. *The Elements of Style*, **4th edition. Needham Heights, MA: Allyn & Bacon, 2000. [105 pp]**

This classic book provides readers with invaluable advice and instruction on the rules of usage when writing. Chapter 1, "Elementary Rules of Usage," covers the most basic aspects of grammar, including the use of commas, colons, and dashes. Chapter 2, "Elementary Principles of Composition," discusses topics such as the construction of paragraphs, the use of the active voice, the need to "omit needless words," and how to construct an effective and clear sentence. Chapter 3 deals with use of colloquialisms, exclamations, headings, margins, quotations, references, and other elements of "form." Chapter 4 covers "commonly misused" words and expressions, providing their definitions and the correct words that should be used in their place.

In Chapter 5, "An Approach to Style (With a List of Reminders)," the authors give more general

advice on writing style, namely, the need to revise and rewrite and to be clear when writing.

Turabian, Kate L. *A Manual for Writers of Research Papers, Theses, and Dissertations*, revised by Wayne C. Booth, Gregory G. Colomb, and Joseph M. Williams and the University of Chicago Press Editorial Staff, 7th edition. Chicago: University of Chicago Press, 2007. [466 pp]

In three parts and 26 chapters, the latest edition of Turabian's classic work provides a detailed

description of the research and writing process. Part I, "Research and Writing: From Planning to

Production," focuses on describing "what research is," the process of going from choosing a

topic to a research question and then to a hypothesis, finding relevant sources, taking effective

notes, "planning an argument," and writing and revising a draft, as well as presenting research

(oral presentation, poster session, conference presentation). Part II, "Source Citation," covers the

different citation styles and the proper citation format (notes and bibliography/reference page).

Part III, "Style," covers items such as spelling, punctuation, names, numbers, abbreviations,

quotations, and tables and figures. The appendix provides an explanation of formatting (margins,

space, pagination, etc), parts of a paper (front and back matter, text), and "submission

requirements" (preparing and submitting hard and electronic copies). The bibliography provides

internet databases and print and electronic resources (i.e., general, humanities, social sciences,

natural sciences).

Turabian, Kate L. *Student's Guide to Writing College Papers*, **revised by Gregory G. Colomb and Joseph M. Williams and the University of Chicago Press Editorial Staff, 4th edition. Chicago: University of Chicago Press, 2010. [281 pp]**

A shorter version of Turabian's *A Manual for Writers*, this book is also divided into three parts: "Writing your Paper," "Citing Sources," and "Style." Part I is focused on asking the question "What researchers do and how do they think about it"? From there, chapters focus on finding a research question, getting good sources, argument, drafts, using sources (paraphrasing versus plagiarism), using tables and figures in a paper, revision, and editing. The second part focuses on the three main citation styles (Chicago, MLA, and APA). The third and final part addresses grammatical issues such as punctuation, spelling, and use of titles, names, and numbers. An appendix (Appendix C) provides excellent Internet databases and print resources for research and writing divided into general, humanities, social sciences, and natural sciences. These four areas are further divided into specific disciplines (history, art, anthropology, economics, etc.).

Bibliography

"About Project Muse." http://muse.jhu.edu/.

Academic OneFile. Accessed May 27, 2011.

     http://www.gale.cengage.com/PeriodicalSolutions/academicOnefile.htm.

Ackerly, Brooke, and Jacqui True. *Doing Feminist Research in Political and Social Science*. New York: Palgrave Macmillan, 2010.

American National Election Studies. www.electionstudies.org.

American Political Science Association. *Style Manual for Political Science*, rev. ed. Washington, DC: American Political Science Association, 2001.

---. "What Is Political Science?" Accessed May 24, 2011.

     http://apsanet.org/content_9181.cfm?navID=727.

American Psychological Association. "How do you cite two or more references within the same parentheses?" Accessed May 24, 2013.

     http://www.apastyle.org/learn/faqs/references-in-parentheses.aspx

---. "Quick Answers-References: Websites." Accessed June 3, 2013.

     http://www.apastyle.org/learn/quick-guide-on-references.aspx#Websites.

Baglione, Lisa A. *Writing a Research Paper in Political Science: A Practical Guide to Inquiry, Structure, and Methods*. Belmont, CA: Thomson Wadsworth, 2007.

Berger, Peter L. "The Cultural Dynamics of Globalization." In *Many Globalizations: Cultural Diversity in the Contemporary World*, edited by Peter L. Berger and Samuel P. Huntington, 1–16. Oxford: Oxford University Press, 2002.

Berger, Peter. L., and Samuel P. Huntington, eds. *Many Globalizations: Cultural Diversity in the Contemporary World*. Oxford: Oxford University Press, 2002.

Booth, Wayne G., Gregory G. Colomb, and Joseph M. Williams. *The Craft of Research*. 3rd ed. Chicago: University of Chicago Press, 2008.

Carlson, James M., and Mark S. Hyde. *Doing Empirical Political Research*. Boston: Houghton Mifflin, 2003.

Cavdar, Gamze, and Sue Doe. "Learning Through Writing: Teaching Critical Thinking Skills in Writing Assignments." *PS: Political Science & Politics* 45, 2 (April 2012): 298–306.

Charlton, Lucille, and Mark Charlton. *Thomson Nelson Guide to Research and Writing in Political Science*. Toronto: Nelson, 2006.

CSA Worldwide Political Science Abstracts. "Fact Sheets." http://www.csa.com/factsheets/polsci.set-c.php.

Di Giovanni, Janine. "The Making of a Monster." *TIME*. June 6, 2011.

Digital National Security Archive. *The National Security Archive*. Accessed June 12, 2011. nsarchive.chadwyck.com/marketing/index.jsp.

Doyle, Michael W. "Liberalism and World Politics." *American Political Science Review* 80 (December 1986): 1151–69.

European Commission. "Public Opinion." Accessed May 14, 2013. http://ec.europa.eu/public_opinion/index.en.htm.

Expanded Academic ASAP. Accessed May 27, 2011. http://www.gale.cengage.com/PeriodicalSolutions/academicAsap.htm?grid=ExpandedAcademicASAPRedirect.

Gibaldi, Joseph. *MLA Handbook for Writers of Research Papers*. 5th ed. New York:

    Modern Language Association of America, 1999.

Gorman, Siobhan. "Cyberspies Target China Experts." *Wall Street Journal*. June 6,

    2001, A4.

Grieco, Joseph. *Cooperation Among Nations: Europe, America, and Non-Tariff Barriers

    to Trade*. Ithaca, NY: Cornell University Press, 1990.

Hochschild, Jennifer L. "Writing Introductions." In *Publishing Political Science: APSA

    Guide to Writing and Publishing*, edited by Stephen Yoder, 93-100. Washington, DC:

    American Political Science Association, 2008.

Ikenberry, G. John. "The Future of the Liberal World Order: Internationalism after

    America." *Foreign Affairs* 90, 3 (May/June 2011): 56–68.

Inter-university Consortium for Political and Social Research. "About ICPSR."

    http://www.icpsr.umich.edu/icpsrweb/content/membership/about.html.

Jones, Jeffrey M. "Gender Gap in 2012 Vote Is Largest in Gallup's History." November

    9, 2012. http://www.gallup.com/poll/158588/gender-gap-2012-vote-largest-

    gallup-history.aspx?.

JSTOR. "About: 10 Things." Accessed May 15, 2013. http://about.jstor.org/10things.

Kane, Thomas S. *The Oxford Essential Guide to Writing*. New York: Berkley Books,

    2000.

Kaufmann, Karen M. "The Gender Gap." *PS: Political Science and Politics* (July 2006):

    447-53.

Keohane, Robert O., and Lisa L. Martin. "The Promise of Institutionalist Theory."

    International Security 20 (1995): 39-51.

Knopf, Jeffrey W., and Iain McMenamin. "How to Write a Literature Review." In

    Publishing Political Science: APSA Guide to Writing and Publishing, edited by Stephen

    Yoder, 101-16. Washington, DC: American Political Science Association, 2008.

Layne, Christopher. "From Preponderance to Offshore Balancing: America's Future

    Grand Strategy." *International Security* 22, 1 (Summer 1997): 86–124.

LexisNexis Academic. "Product Overview." Accessed May 31, 2011.

    http://academic.lexisnexis.com/online-services/academic/academic-overview.aspx.

Library of Congress. "American Women: The General Collections." Accessed May 31,

    2011. http://memory.loc.gov/ammem/awhhtml/awgc1/index.html.

---. "Using Primary Sources." Accessed May 31, 2011.

    http://www.loc.gov/teachers/usingprimarysources/.

Lipson, Charles. *How to Write a BA Thesis: A Practical Guide from Your First Ideas to*

    Your Finished Paper. Chicago: University of Chicago Press, 2005.

McCoy, Amanda. "Writing a Strong Essay Introduction." March 2, 2010. Accessed June 3,

    2013. http://suite101.com/article/writing-a-strong-essay-introduction-a208370.

Mearsheimer, John J. "The False Promise of International Institutions." *International*

    Security 19 (Winter 1994/1995): 5–49.

---. *The Tragedy of Great Power Politics.* New York: W.W. Norton,

    2001.

Meernik, James D., Angela Nichols, and Kimi L. King. "The Impact of International

    Tribunals and Domestic Trials on Peace and Human Rights after Civil War."

    International Studies Perspectives 11, 4 (2010): 309–34.

MLA Handbook for Writers of Research Papers. 7th ed. New York: Modern Language

Association of America, 2009.

PAIS International and PAIS Archives. "Fact Sheets." Accessed May 31, 2011.

http://www.csa.com/factsheets/pais-set-c.php.

Patrick, Stewart. *Weak Links: Fragile States, Global Threats, and International Security*.

New York: Oxford University Press, 2011.

Peterson, V. Spike. "Feminist Theories Within, Invisible to, and Beyond IR." *Brown

Journal of World Affairs* X, 2 (Winter/Spring 2004): 35–46.

---. "Plural Processes, Patterned Connections." *Globalizations* 1, 1 (September 2004):

50–68.

Purdue Online Writing Lab. "Reference List: Basic Rules: APA Style." Purdue

University. Accessed May 23, 2013. http://owl.english.purdue.edu/owl/resource/560/05/.

Rae, Tushar. "E-Books' Varied Formats Make Citations a Mess for Scholars."

Chronicle of Higher Education. February 6, 2011. Accessed May 9, 2011.

http://chronicle.com/article/E-Books-Varied-Formats-Make/126246/.

Rael, Patrick. *Reading, Writing, and Researching for History: A Guide for College

Students*. Brunswick, ME: Bowdoin College, 2004. Accessed June 3, 2013.

http://www.bowdoin.edu/writing-guides/sample%20road%20map.htm.

Regan, Patrick. M., and Daniel Norton. "Greed, Grievance, and Mobilization in Civil

Wars." *The Journal of Conflict Resolution* 49, 3 (June 2005): 319–36.

Roselle, Laura, and Sharon Spray. *Research and Writing in International Relations*. New

York: Pearson Longman, 2008.

Schmidt, Diane E. *Writing in Political Science: A Practical Guide*. 4th ed. New York:

    Pearson Longman, 2010.

Schweller, Randall. "Unanswered Threats: A Neoclassical Realist Theory of

    Underbalancing." *International Security* 29, 2 (Fall 2004): 159–201.

Scott, Gregory M., and Stephen M. Garrison. *The Political Science Student Writer's*

    Manual. 7th ed. New York: Pearson Longman, 2012.

Sherman, Will. "33 Reasons Why Libraries and Librarians Are Still Extremely

    Important." *Library News*. February 1, 2007. Accessed May 14, 2013.

    http://greatlibrarynews.blogspot.ca/2007/02/33-reasons-why-libraries-and.html.

Singer, David J. "International Conflict: Three Levels of Analysis." *World Politics* 12,

    3 (April 1960): 453–461.

---. "The Level-of-Analysis Problem in International Relations." *World Politics* 14, 1

    (October 1961): 77–92.

Sperling, Valerie. "Review [untitled]." Women's Access to Political Power in Post-

    Communist Europe. Edited by Richard E. Matland and Kathleen A. Montogomery. New

    York: Oxford University Press, 2003. In *Perspectives on Politics* 2, 4 (December 2004):

    878–79.

Spiegel, Steven L. Elizabeth G. Matthews, Jennifer M. Taw, and Kristen P. Williams.

    World Politics in a New Era, 5th ed. New York: Oxford University Press, 2012.

Strunk, William Jr., and E. B. White. *The Elements of Style*, 4th ed. New York: Longman

    Publishing, 2000.

"Thinking Critically About World Wide Web Resources." Created by Esther Grassian, the
    UCLA Library and used with permission. June 1995. Accessed May 11, 2011.
    http://www2.library.ucla.edu/libraries/college/11605_12337.cfm.

Towns, Ann E. *Women and States: Norms and Hierarchies in International Society*. New
    York: Cambridge University Press, 2010.

Turabian, Kate L. *A Manual for Writers of Research Papers, Theses, and Dissertations*.
    7th ed. Revised by Wayne C. Booth, Gregory G. Colomb, and Joseph M. Williams and
    the University of Chicago Editorial Press Staff. Chicago: University of Chicago Press,
    2007.

---. *Student's Guide to Writing College Papers*, 4th ed. Revised by Gregory G. Colomb, Joseph
    M. Williams, and the University of Chicago Press Editorial Staff. Chicago: University of
    Chicago Press, 2010.

United Nations. "United Nations Declaration of Human Rights."
    http://www.un.org/en/documents/udhr/index.shtml.

University of Chicago Press. *The Chicago Manual of Style: The Essential Guide for
    Writers, Editors, and Publishers*. 16th ed. Chicago: University of Chicago Press, 2010.

University of Maryland, University Libraries. "Primary, Secondary and Tertiary
    Sources." Accessed May 31, 2011. http://www.lib.umd.edu/guides/primary-sources.html.

U.S. Agency for International Development. "Conflict Mitigation and Prevention."
    Accessed May 27, 2013. http://www.usaid.gov/what-we-do/working-crises-and-
    conflict/conflict-mitigation-and-prevention.

U.S. Census Bureau. www.census.gov.

U.S. Congressional Serial Set. www.gpo.gov/help/u.s._congressional_serial_set.htm.

Van Evera, Stephen. *Guide to Methods for Students of Political Science*. Ithaca, NY: Cornell

    University Press, 1997.

Walt, Stephen M. *The Origins of Alliances*. Ithaca, NY: Cornell University Press, 1987.

Waltz, Kenneth N. *Man, the State and War: A Theoretical Analysis*. New York:

    Columbia University Press, 1959.

---. *Theory of International Politics*. New York: Random House, 1979.

Wendt, Alexander. "Anarchy Is What States Make of It: The Social Construction of

    Power Politics." *International Organization* 46, 2 (Spring 1992): 391–425.

"What's Wrong with Wikipedia?" Harvard Guide to Using Sources, Harvard College

    Writing Program. Accessed February 25, 2013.

    http://isites.harvard.edu/icb/icb.do?keyword=k70847&pageid=icb.page346376.

"Wikipedia: No Original Research." *Wikipedia*. Accessed February 25, 2013.

    http://simple.wikipedia.org/wiki/Wikipedia:No_original_research.

World Bank. http://www.worldbank.org.

CPSIA information can be obtained at www.ICGtesting.com
Printed in the USA
LVOW03s0004180715

446577LV00002B/3/P

9 780199 890545